THE IDIOM OF THE PEOPLE

JAMES REEVES

THE IDIOM OF THE PEOPLE

English Traditional Verse

EDITED
WITH AN INTRODUCTION
AND NOTES
FROM THE MANUSCRIPTS OF
CECIL J. SHARP

faber and faber

This edition first published in 2008
by Faber and Faber Ltd
3 Queen Square, London WC1N 3AU

Printed by Books on Demand GmbH, Norderstedt

All rights reserved
© James Reeves, 1958

The right of James Reeves to be identified as editor of this work
has been asserted in accordance with Section 77 of the
Copyright, Designs and Patents Act 1988

This book is sold subject to the condition that it shall not, by way of
trade or otherwise, be lent, resold, hired out or otherwise circulated
without the publisher's prior consent in any form of binding or cover other than
that in which it is published and without a similar condition including this
condition being imposed on the subsequent purchaser

A CIP record for this book is available from the British Library

ISBN 978–0–571–24570–3

TO ROBERT AND BERYL
WITH LOVE

CONTENTS

INDEX OF SONGS	ix
ACKNOWLEDGMENTS	xii
INTRODUCTION	
1. The Folk Song Movement in England	1
2. Cecil Sharp as Folk Song Collector	4
3. The Revision of Folk Song Words	8
4. The Sharp Manuscripts	17
5. The Idiom of the People	23
6. Some Folk Songs Considered	33
NOTE ON THE TEXT	60
ENGLISH TRADITIONAL VERSE:	
TEXT AND NOTES	61
INDEX OF FIRST LINES	242

LIST OF PLATES

		Facing page
1.	O No John (No. 68)	36
2.	Waly Waly (No. 108)	37
3.	Blow away the Morning Dew (No. 14)	52
4.	The Foggy Dew (No. 33).	53

INDEX OF SONGS

1. Adieu to Old England 61
2. An Alderman's Lady 62
3. The Alphabet 63
4. American Stranger 64
5. Arthur Bradley O 66
6. As I walked through the Meadows 68
7. As I was going to Banbury 69

8. Banks of Claudy 70
9. The Banks of Green Willow 72
10. The Basket of Eggs 73
11. Bessy Bingle 74
12. Billy Boy 75
13. Bird Starver's Cry 76
14. Blow away the Morning Dew 77
15. Blow the Wind Whistling 82
16. The Boatman and the Tailor 83
17. The Bold Grenadier 85
18. Bold Robinson 87
19. The Brisk Young Bachelor 88
20. A Brisk Young Lover 90
21. The Broomfield Wager 93
22. Cold Blow and a Rainy Night 96

23. The Cuckoo 97

24. Dabbling in the Dew 100
25. The Dandy Man 101
26. The Derby Ram 102
27. The Devil's in the Girl 104
28. Down by a River Side 106
29. No my Love not I 108
30. I'm a Day too Young 109
31. Down in my Garden 110

32. The Female Cabin Boy no 110
33. The Foggy Dew in 111

34. Gently Johnny my Jingalo 113
35. The German Flute 115
36. Good Old Man 115
37. Gossip Joan 117

THE IDIOM OF THE PEOPLE

38 Hares on the Mountains   119
39 A Harvest Song   121
40 Haymaking Courtship   122
41 The Hazelbury Girl   123
42 Hacketty Pecketty   125
43 High Germany   125
44 I'm Seventeen Come Sunday   127
45 I Sowed some Seeds   128
46 I've been a Roving   129
47 I Wish I had never Known   129
48 The Irish Girl   130
49 Jack Hall   132
50 Joan's Ale was New   133
51 Jolly Old Hawk   136
52 The Keeper   138
53 The Kettle Smock   139
54 The Keys of Heaven   140
55 Lancashire Lass   144
56 The Lark in the Morn   145
57 The London, Man of War   146
58 Long and Wishing Eye   148
59 Lord Thomas of Winesberry   149
60 The Lowlands of Holland   151
61 Maid Freed from the Gallows   153
62 Man of War   155
63 The Miller and the Lass   156
64 Mowing the Barley   157
65 My Bonny Bonny Boy   158
66 My Valentine   159
67 O Dear O   160
68 O No John   162
69 Ripest Apples   163
70 On Monday Morning I Married a Wife   164
71 Our Captain cried All Hands   165
72 Our Goodman   167
73 Pery Mery Winkle Domine   169
74 Poaching Song   170
75 Poor Nell   171
76 The Poor Old Couple   174
77 Poor Old Horse   175

x

INDEX OF SONGS

78 The Rambling Boy 178
79 The Red Herring 179
80 The Rigs of London Town 180
81 Rosemary Lane 181
82 Rout of the Blues 184
83 The Rover 185
84 The Roving Journeyman 186

85 The Sailor and the Soldier 187
86 Sailor Cut Down in his Prime 188
87 Sailors they are such a Sort 189
88 Salisbury Plain 189
89 The Sea Captain 191
90 Searching for Lambs 192
91 The Seeds of Love 194
92 The Sentry 197
93 Sheep Stealer 198
94 The Sign of the Bonny Blue Bell 198
95 Single Men's Warning 199
96 Still Growing 200
97 Sweet Primaroses 202

98 The Tailor by his Trade 203
99 There was an Old Woman 204
100 The Thrashing Machine 206
101 The Three Cripples 207
102 Three Maids a Milking 208
103 Three Maids a Rushing 210
104 The Tree in the Wood 211
105 The Turtle Dove 213
106 The Two Jovial Butchers 215

107 Van Dieman's Land 217

108 Waly Waly 218
109 Well Done Liar 220
110 When shall we get Married 221
111 Whistle Daughter Whistle 223
112 The Wife of Usher's Well 225
113 William Taylor 227
114 Willie's Courtship 230

115 Young Barns well 230

Appendix of additional songs and fragments 233

ACKNOWLEDGMENTS

I wish to acknowledge my indebtedness to the following and to offer my sincerest thanks for their help: to Miss Maud Karpeles, both for her assistance on various points and for permission to reprint copyright material; to the Master and Fellows of Clare College, Cambridge, for permission to examine and make transcriptions from the Sharp Collection in the Forbes Library, and to make photographic reproductions of several pages; and especially to the former Deputy Librarian, Dr J. R. Northam, for his unwearied hospitality while I was working at Cambridge, and to Dr F. Brittain of Jesus College for his generous entertainment during the same period; to the photographic staff of the University Library; to Messrs Novello and Co. Ltd., to the Oxford University Press, and to Messrs Methuen and Co. Ltd, for permission to quote from copyright material published by them; to Mrs Sally Chilver, Mr Richard Fairbairn and the Librarian of the English Folk Dance and Song Society for the loan of books and journals; to Mr Richard Ludwig of Princeton University, to Mr Anthony Crowe, Mr Brian Jackson and Mr Stephen Pike of St Catharine's College, Cambridge, for help in reading and transcribing the mss., and to Mr John Harris, also of St Catharine's, and Miss Valerie Little of Somerville College, Oxford, for assistance in transcribing and editing the songs; to the following for valuable suggestions and information in answer to my numerous enquiries: Mrs Marjorie Barnett, Mr Benjamin Britten, Mrs R. Bromwich, Dr Donald Davie, Miss Margaret Dean-Smith (whose *Guide to English Folk Song Collections* has proved indispensable), Mr Seámus Ennis, Mr Robert Graves, Mr Christopher Middleton, Mr Eric Partridge, Mr Patrick Shuldham-Shaw, the Librarian of the National Maritime Museum, Greenwich, and the staff of the Reading Room at the British Museum; and to Mrs Dorothy Glen, Mr Geoffrey Marwood and Mrs Mary Reeves for reading and correcting the typescript. I wish also to express my gratitude to the writers of other works quoted in the introduction and notes.

J.R.

Introduction

I

THE FOLK SONG MOVEMENT IN ENGLAND

WHEN Herder, in 1773, first brought the word *Volkslied* into literary use, he was concerned primarily with folk poetry, not music. A century later, when the English folk song movement which culminated in the work of Cecil Sharp was under way, the position was reversed. During the late eighteenth and early nineteenth centuries, though some interest was shown, especially in Scotland, in traditional-airs, the main concern of collectors such as Scott and the members of the Percy Society was with ballad words. It was not until well on in the nineteenth century that musical antiquarians like William Chappell made it widely understood that traditional poetry had tunes as well as words. Collections of 'peasant' songs began to appear, in which both words and music were given, and by the middle of the century such collectors as John Broadwood and J. H. Dixon had published texts actually transcribed from the lips of unlettered country people.

These early collections were printed for limited circulation only, and were sponsored by antiquarian societies. Perhaps the earliest attempt towards a great national collection, for national circulation, was that begun in the late 1880's by the Rev. Sabine Baring-Gould and his associates. The 'nineties saw the publication of collections by Frank Kidson, Lucy Broadwood and others; and about this time the movement for preserving the songs of the people took on a missionary spirit. Enthusiasts began to compare the songs they had rescued with the debased productions of composers for the drawing-room, the concert hall and the music hall. The improvement of national taste became a conscious aim. To preserve the musical heritage of the past, and to reform the musical taste of the present was the twofold object.

In 1898 the unco-ordinated efforts of enthusiastic individuals coalesced in the foundation of the Folk-Song Society. It was

THE IDIOM OF THE PEOPLE

essentially a musical organization. Its first Vice-Presidents were Sir John Stainer, Mr C. V. Stanford, Sir A. C. Mackenzie and Sir Hubert Parry, all of whom held high public offices in music. The Committee contained several folk song collectors, including Lucy Broadwood and Frank Kidson. There were about a hundred members, of whom some were interested in folk lore but none was eminent in literature. The first general meeting was held in London on February 2nd, 1899. One of the rules adopted was:

> The Society shall have for its primary object the collection and preservation of folk-songs, ballads, and tunes, and the publication of such of these as may be deemed advisable.

The inaugural address was given by Sir Hubert Parry, who voiced the missionary spirit then prevalent, and set the tone for the official English folk song movement of the next two decades. Modern commercialism, he said, was tending to make us cynical about our fellow creatures; but a better view must prevail among 'those who study folk-music; for one of the strangest things about it is that there is nothing in it common or unclean'. He goes on to ask, 'How has the unregenerate public arrived at such a happy result that in true folk-songs there is no sham, no got-up glitter, and no vulgarity?'

The Folk-Song Society, now The English Folk Dance and Song Society, has continued in existence from that day until now. It has formed a focus for the activities of collectors and exponents of these traditional arts, and has set high standards. Its work in the several related fields of its activities has been of the utmost value. Its annual journals are a repository of texts and information which might otherwise have been irretrievably lost. The failings exhibited by the Society at its beginning, over half a century ago, have long since been remedied. Yet it is worth while to dwell briefly on some aspects of that beginning, in view of their effect on the subsequent history of folk song publication during the life of Cecil Sharp. First, it was launched by a very distinguished gathering of musical knights and professors; it met, not in a public-house or a barn in the country, but in a Mayfair drawing-room; and its official attitude, whatever the private habits of mind of its individual members, was patronizing. Such a society, founded when it was, was bound to be of this character. Above all, it was a musicians' society.

For the purposes of this introduction, what was the attitude of the members of the Folk-Song Society to the words of the songs they collected? For however exclusively interested some of them may have been in music, they found themselves, in their visits to country villages, confronted with a twofold phenomenon—words and melody. The musician's standpoint was well expressed by a founding Committee member, Frank Kidson, in the Preface to his *Traditional Tunes* (Oxford, 1891). It was the melodies that interested him, and the words were often transcribed from broadsides and heavily censored. His attitude was one of admiration marred by patronage.

> The songs here given are simply homely ditties such as were sung by the humbler classes in England round the fireside of farm kitchens or at the plough tail, and the little wit or brilliancy they may possess must not be judged by a very high standard.

He goes on to speak of the rapidity with which the old songs were dying out, a conclusion arrived at by every collector of folk songs from the first half of the nineteenth century to the present day.

> The old traditional songs are fast dying out, never to be recalled. They are now seldom or never sung, but rather *remembered*, by old people.

Kidson's final judgment on the words of folk songs must also be quoted, since it was adopted as a common-place by almost the entire movement:

> It must also be conceded that the rustic muse produced better melody than poetry or even rhyme.

In the Introduction to the 1905 edition of his *Songs of the West*, Baring-Gould was even more disdainful of the words as contrasted with the airs. Sharp, in an article in the *Journal of the Folk-Song Society* for the same year, said with greater moderation:

> My own estimate is that the tunes are of the utmost value, but that the words are of less account.

This is the view which still obtains. Sharp's official biographers, for instance, wrote:

> It is unfortunate that the words of the folk-songs which have come down to us are not, generally speaking, on the same artistic level as the tunes,

although there are notable exceptions, for example, 'O Waly, Waly', 'Searching for Lambs', and 'Scarborough Fair'.[1]

A reason for this state of affairs is suggested by the writer of the article on Folk Song in the *Oxford Companion to Music* (1938):

> ... it may be observed that, although many lovely and sensitive folk poems exist, yet as a body the tunes are finer than their words, education being more of a factor in the production of a poem than of a tune.

2
CECIL SHARP AS FOLK SONG COLLECTOR

Cecil Sharp was not one of the founders of the Society, but before long he was an active and critical member. Born in London in 1859, and educated at Uppingham School and Clare College, Cambridge, he led a varied musical life in Australia and England. He suffered from chronic asthma, and it was not till comparatively late in his life that he was free from financial anxiety. He came into contact with English morris dancing and with folk singing during visits to the west country in holidays from teaching. At the time of his discovery of folk songs he was Principal of the Hampstead Conservatoire of Music. At about this time he joined the Folk-Song Society, against which he launched a vigorous attack early in 1904. The Society, he said, was moribund, and had done nothing it set out to do except publish about a hundred songs in successive issues of its journal. Above all, it had not co-ordinated the individual efforts of its members, and the purposed campaign to collect and preserve the national heritage of song remained spasmodic and inadequate. Sharp was elected to the Committee of the Society, and the sixth number of its journal, issued in 1905, was devoted to an article by him, together with some twenty-nine songs he had noted in Somerset and North Devon.

Meanwhile, an occurrence had taken place whose implications were of immense importance for Sharp and the folk song movement. The Board of Education had discovered Folk Music. Its

---
[1] A. H. Fox Strangways and Maud Karpeles: *Cecil Sharp* (1933, second edition 1955).

CECIL SHARP AS FOLK SONG COLLECTOR

annual *Handbook of Suggestions for the Consideration of Teachers* reflected official opinion as to the methods and content of elementary education in Britain, and was (and still is) of paramount importance in guiding national practice in the schools. The Handbook for 1905, in its chapter on 'The Teaching of Singing', contained the following:

> By wisely chosen songs the natural play of the healthy emotions of childhood can find an expression at once ample and controlled....
>
> National or folk songs . . . are the expression in the idiom of the people of their joys and sorrows, their unaffected patriotism, their zest for sport and the simple pleasures of a country life. Such music is the early and spontaneous uprising of artistic power in a nation, and the ground on which all national music is built up; folk-songs are the true classics of a people, and their survival, so often by tradition alone, proves that their appeal is direct and lasting. . . .
>
> Some of the folk-music of England, Scotland, Ireland, and Wales is unsuitable either in words or in compass for the use of schools, and care must therefore be taken in making a choice. . . .
>
> The songs chosen for infants should be musically as simple as possible; but it is not necessary that infants should understand all the words they sing, as the chief appeal is not to the intellect, the training of which is the purpose of almost every other subject in the curriculum, but through the spirit of the song to the unconscious mind of the child. . . .

It is not necessary for present purposes to criticize in detail this official pronouncement. It was seized on by Sharp as a warrant for the educational campaign he was to begin immediately. But first there was an important preliminary battle to be fought. He felt obliged to establish, with the maximum of publicity, the true nature of 'folk' as distinct from 'national' song. A spirited and acrimonious controversy was waged in the public press for and against Sharp's views, a controversy now of merely historical importance. Sharp's contention was that there is an essential difference between an authentic, traditional song of the kind he had been noting in Somerset from the lips of villagers, and 'composed' songs like *Tom Bowling* and *Rule Britannia*. He believed that the former were musically far superior, and it became his principal aim to get these established in the musical consciousness of the nation at large through the elementary schools. Musical opinion has since endorsed his view. By a characteristically British compromise folk songs have not replaced 'national' songs in the school repertoire, but been added to them.

THE IDIOM OF THE PEOPLE

It is clear that throughout the course of the controversy both Sharp and his critics assumed that they were talking about music, not poetry. But when in 1907 Sharp found time to publish his interim report on the subject of folk songs in general,[1] he referred to the words of the songs; and he may have been thinking of the remarks quoted above from the Board of Education's Handbook when he observed, justly, that the true folk song had little concern with patriotism or sport. The outlaw was, he said, more popular than the hero—Robin Hood was preferred to Nelson. As for sport, folk songs were little preoccupied with the pursuits of the gentry, preferring poaching to fox-hunting. Again, praise of the home and of domestic life, Sharp remarked, was not among the themes of true folk song. The widespread popularity of *The Raggle-Taggle Gypsies* was significant. It may be observed that Sharp was free from the taint of snobbery and patronage which had marked the attitude of some nineteenth-century collectors. He had a strong strain of progressive radicalism, and the contrary tendency—that of sentimentalizing the poor and humble—was a more common one in the early days of Fabian Socialism. It is recorded that as an undergraduate Sharp used to propose annually at the meetings of the College debating society a motion to abolish the House of Lords. The interest in folk song shown by Sharp and his contemporaries was primarily musical, but also social: folk song was worth preserving *because* it was popular. Even official pronouncements, as we have seen, paid lip-service to this idea.

The cultural movement associated with Sharp's name is threefold: the effort of his life work was directed towards the collecting and publishing of English folk songs, the revival of morris dancing, and the collecting of songs in America. Only the first of these is our present concern. The event which determined the main direction of his efforts and fired his missionary and propagandist zeal was the visit he paid in September 1903 to the vicarage of his friend, the Rev. Charles L. Marson, at Hambridge in Somerset. The two men shared a common interest in folk song, though neither had as yet studied it in its living form. Both were amazed at the quantity and quality of the songs they discovered the moment they began to dig beneath the surface. Marson in particular was surprised that the thing had gone on under his nose, so to speak, while as vicar he had

---
[1] Cecil J. Sharp: *English Folk Songs: Some Conclusions* (London, 1907).

remained in ignorance of it. Indeed, the very first folk song taken down by Sharp and preserved on the opening page of his notebooks was from the lips of the vicar's own gardener, a man with the remarkably symbolic name of John England. The song was *The Seeds of Love.*

> Sharp whipped out his notebook, took down the tune, and afterwards persuaded John to give him the words. He went off and harmonized the song, and that same evening it was sung at a choir supper by Mattie Kay, Sharp accompanying. The audience was delighted; as one said, it was the first time that the song had been put into evening-dress. John was proud, but doubtful about the 'evening-dress'; there had been no piano to *his* song.[1]

It would be a mistake to inflate the importance of this occurrence, yet certain features do invite comment: tune first—then words; harmonization for the piano; performance at the church supper. The significance of these circumstances for the student of traditional poetry, as preserved in Sharp's notebooks, will appear later. They reveal much of the process by which, despite Sharp's instincts to the contrary, a folk product was turned, to a considerable extent, into an art product.

From that moment on, Sharp took every possible opportunity to listen to and transcribe the songs of the country people in Somerset and neighbouring districts. Despite other preoccupations, which crowded in on him as life went on, he continued to collect English folk songs until the year of his death, 1924. He was, as he admitted, a man of somewhat autocratic temperament, an individualist impatient of delay, obstruction and stupidity. Yet the patience he displayed in the pursuit of his principal object—the preservation of the English musical heritage—was unsurpassed. His energy in search of good singers and songs was, despite his chronic asthma, inexhaustible. His notebooks, which will be referred to in detail later, are a unique storehouse of verse and melody. Some, perhaps much, of it would have been lost for ever if he had not saved it. Sharp's achievement was manifold, but I believe that his greatest and most indisputable contribution was made as a collector. To his painstaking accuracy in transcription, as well as to the labours of other pioneers, we owe the existence of so much material that can only now for the first time be made public. That it could not be made

[1] Fox Strangways and Karpeles: *op. cit.*

public during his lifetime was no fault of Sharp's. Why this should be so must now be considered.

3

THE REVISION OF FOLK SONG WORDS

It had long been known to editors of songs from the 'peasantry', as they had formerly been called, that while the tunes were often of rare beauty and purity, the words were far from acceptable to the taste of the polite world. Dialect usages were common, and grammar was often so unconventional as to be ludicrous. Worse still, there were in traditional verse none of the taboos, especially with regard to sex, which were taken for granted in the public utterance of the educated. Nor was it simply a matter of taboos in the negative sense. Not only did folk songs contain overt references to fornication and pregnancy; there was a quite shameless delight and interest in the details of these matters. Not only was there little or none of the archness and evasion characteristic of courtship among the refined, both in life and in song, there was a sense of unregenerate pagan enjoyment of natural functions in love and courtship, and a lack of reticence in expressing the pleasures and pains of exercising them. Despite the efforts of puritans to suppress all this, it had persisted; and the evangelical churches in the nineteenth century had combated, or at least frowned on, the public expression of anything unfit for a choir supper.

The early and mid-nineteenth century was almost as innocent in its suppression of what it considered 'rude' or 'gross' as the peasantry were in clinging to it. There were taboos—and that was that. No printer would undertake to reproduce certain verses verbatim,[1]

---

[1] This of course does not apply to the printers of ballad-sheets and street songs. Compare Henry Mayhew's interview with 'A Street Author or Poet' (*London Labour and the London Poor*, 1851):

'Above fourteen years ago I tried to make a shilling or two by selling my verses. I'd written plenty before, but made nothing by them. Indeed I never tried. The first song I ever sold was to a concert room manager. The next I sold had great success. It was called the "Demon of the Sea", and was to the tune of "The Brave Old Oak". . . . I have written all sorts of things—ballads on a subject, and copies of verses, and anything ordered of me, or on anything I thought would be accepted, but now I can't get about. I've been asked to

and no publisher of repute would issue them, so the editor had no alternative but to omit or alter the offending verses. This was so much the common practice that no one seemed to question its propriety, and it was not until the later nineteenth century that editors usually recorded the facts of their re-writing. It is possible that Baring-Gould was the last great editor to expurgate without a qualm. The sort of phrases which abound in his editorial notes are 'objectionable', 'not very choice', 'impossible to print', 'too coarse for reproduction', 'very indelicate', 'very gross', and 'The coarseness of the original words obliged me to re-write the song'. Unfortunately the mere 'softening', as it was called, of offensive words and phrases was not always sufficient; the entire situation celebrated by a song might be unacceptable. So that in their zeal for getting good tunes known and sung editors like Baring-Gould felt no compunction in supplying a whole set of words entirely composed by themselves. In this way the wild flower was domesticated beyond recognition; the folk song became the art song.

This was basically the situation inherited by Sharp when in the winter of 1903 he and Marson began to edit for the general public the songs collected at Hambridge. In 1904 appeared the first collection of *Folk Songs from Somerset*, a series of five volumes Sharp edited (the first three in collaboration with Marson) between that year and 1909. This first collection was 'Dedicated by permission to Her Royal Highness the Princess of Wales'—that is, Queen Mary— to whose children Sharp gave musical instruction at Marlborough House from 1904 to 1907. Even if there had been no other consideration, clearly the publication must obey the strictest canons of propriety. Even so, Marson's remarks in the Introduction show signs of regret that things were as they were:

> Folk song, unknown in the drawing-room, hunted out of the school, chased by the chapel deacons, derided by the middle classes, and despised by those who have been uneducated into the three R's, takes refuge in the fastnesses of tap-rooms, poor cottages and outlying hamlets.

write indecent songs, but I refused. One man offered me 5s. for six such songs. — "Why, that's less than the common price," said I, "instead of something over to pay for the wickedness."—All those sort of songs come now to the streets, I believe all do, from the concert-rooms. I can imitate any poetry. I don't recollect any poet I've imitated. No, sir, not Scott or Moore, that I know of, but if they've written popular songs, then I daresay I have imitated them.'

THE IDIOM OF THE PEOPLE

He goes on to say that it will soon be extinct even in these places, owing to the flight from the countryside. He continues:

> The collection here made is presented to the public as nearly as possible just as it was taken down from the lips of the singers; in the tunes with exact fidelity. We have not tried to reproduce by spelling the Somerset dialect . . . but anything like a peculiar use, which is characteristic of the speech, we have carefully kept . . .; we have reluctantly changed the weak perfects into the strong ones, but this can easily be *seed* and *knowed* and changed back again by the reader who chooses to do so. In a few instances the sentiment of the song has been softened, because the conventions of our less delicate and more dishonest time demand such treatment, but indication has been given, and we plead compulsion and not desire in these alterations. Things which were obvious slips of grammar we have corrected, but not until all other excuses for them have been tried.

As these remarks indicate, the alterations made in the texts of the songs fell into two main classes: those designed to bring the words into line with conventional usage in grammar and syntax, and those necessitated on grounds of propriety. In their notes to the songs the two editors were on the whole candid about these alterations, though they did not always indicate their extent. Nor could their readers always guess how far the whole character of a song might be altered by only a few slight verbal changes. In his inaugural address to the Folk-Song Society, Parry had spoken of the qualities necessary to enable a collector 'to distinguish what is genuine from what is emasculated'. It is ironical that a man like Sharp, who possessed these qualities in full measure, should, when publishing his discoveries, have been obliged to emasculate them. Such changes were inevitable if the songs were to be offered to the general public; they were even more essential when, in response to the encouragement given by the Board of Education, the songs came to be edited for schools.

But there was another reason for alteration not mentioned by Marson. It will be remembered that *The Seeds of Love* was put into evening-dress and performed at the choir supper. 'Performance', whether in the drawing-room or the classroom, implied accompaniment; at that time this meant, almost invariably, accompaniment on the piano. All the accompaniments were composed by Sharp; and owing to the exigences of music publication and the high cost of engraving, as a rule only the accompaniment to the first verse was

THE REVISION OF FOLK SONG WORDS

given. This was the usual practice. It necessarily destroyed the possibility of observing the subtle rhythmical variations which the folk singers, unaccompanied, were able to make as they sang successive stanzas of a song to the same melody. Sharp records how original and inventive many singers were in this respect. When these songs were set to piano accompaniments, the editor was under the necessity of modifying his texts. The difficulty was expressed clearly enough by another editor, Ethel Kidson, in the Preface to a collection of songs from the mss. of her uncle, Frank Kidson:[1]

> It is the experience of every collector of Folk-Songs that after the first verse the words rarely fit the melody; succeeding verses are often very irregular in metre and are sometimes unsingable. I have endeavoured to put these songs in such a form as to make them acceptable to modern singers, and I have revised many unequal places in the text.

The metrical regularity which has thus been imposed on the words of folk songs has destroyed something of their flexibility and spontaneity. It was the practice, even in Sharp's time, to print unaccompanied melodies in the *Journal of the Folk-Song Society*, and this has since become the general rule, except where a commercial publication is concerned. However, this does not altogether remove the necessity for modifying the words to fit the melody, since modern singers have lost the traditional singer's art, which is more like that of plain-song than accompanied concert performance. In short, while the folk song editor, on commercial considerations, is obliged to fit the words to the tune, it was the habit of traditional folk-singers to fit the tune to the words. In view of Sharp's avowedly overruling interest in the tunes, the following admission is significant:[2]

> It is a well-known fact that the folk-singer attaches far more importance to the words of his song than to its tune; that, while he is conscious of the words that he is singing, he is more or less unconscious of the melody.

For these reasons it is being increasingly recognized that the only authentic way to sing a folk song is unaccompanied. Instrumental accompaniment, even with the singer's own guitar, almost always constitutes a distraction which interferes with a full appreciation of the words.

[1] Frank Kidson: *English Peasant Songs* (London, 1929).
[2] Cecil Sharp: *English Folk Songs, Some Conclusions* (London, 1907).

THE IDIOM OF THE PEOPLE

To return to the question of expurgation—far the most fruitful source of falsification of folk poetry, of distortion of the idiom of the people by the standards of the polite. It is worth while quoting in full what Sharp had to say on this subject:

> Over and above this question of word-corruption, there are some folk-songs, which, for other reasons, can only be published after extensive alteration or excision. Some of these, happily only a few, are gross and coarse in sentiment and objectionable in every way. I am convinced, however, that the majority of these are individual and not communal productions, and cannot therefore be classed as genuine folk-songs. At any rate, I know that they offend against the communal sense of propriety, that the verdict of the community is expressly against them, and that those who sing them do so fully understanding that they are bad, vicious and indefensible.
>
> But there are also a large number of folk-songs, which transgress the accepted conventions of the present age, and which would shock the susceptibilities of those who rank reticence and reserve amongst the noblest of the virtues. These are not, strictly speaking, bad songs; they contain nothing that is really wrong or unwholesome. And they do not violate the communal sense of what is right and proper. They are sung freely and openly by peasant singers, in entire innocence of heart, and without the shadow of a thought that they themselves are committing any offence against propriety in singing them.
>
> This is a phenomenon which opens up a large question. The key-note of folk-poetry, as we have already shown, is simplicity and directness without subtlety—as in the Bible narratives and Shakespeare. This characteristic might be mistaken for a want of refinement by those who live in an age where subtlety and circumlocution are extensively practised. This question comes especially to the fore when the most universal and elemental of all subjects is treated, that of love and the relations of man to woman. Its very intimacy and mystery cause many minds to shrink from expressing themselves openly on the subject, as they would shrink from desecrating a shrine. The ballad-maker has no such feeling. He has none of that delicacy which, as often as not, degenerates into pruriency. Consequently, he treats 'the way of a man with a maid' simply and directly, just as he treats every other subject. Those, therefore, who would study ballad-literature, must realize that they will find in it none of those feelings and unuttered thoughts, which are characteristic of a more self-conscious but by no means more pure-minded age. Nevertheless, however much we may admire the simplicity and straightforward diction of the ballad-maker, we have to realize that other times and other

THE REVISION OF FOLK SONG WORDS

people are not so simple-minded and downright, and what is deemed fit and proper for one period is not necessarily so for others. The folk-song editor, therefore, has perforce to undertake the distasteful task of modifying noble and beautiful sentiments in order that they may suit the minds and conform to the conventions of another age, where such things would not be understood in the primitive, direct and healthy sense.

These songs, however, in that they throw searching light upon the character of the peasant, possess great scientific value. For this reason alone, it is obviously the duty of the collector to note them down conscientiously and accurately, and to take care that his transcriptions are placed in libraries in museums, where they may be examined by students and those who will not misunderstand them.[1]

Sharp was correct in making a distinction between outright bawdry—songs which one singer described to Lucy Broadwood as 'outway rude'—and indelicacy as understood by the polite world. Everyone was united in declining to print texts which were either bawdy or indelicate. Even the Folk-Song Society's *Journal*, issued for circulation among its members only, did not relax its standards until after the 1914–18 war. There is no evidence that any collector was himself (or herself) personally shocked by anything he heard. Sharp was a man of the world and had been a member of his college boat club. Neither were the Anglican clergy who engaged in song-hunting outraged except on behalf of public decency. But such was the strength of habit and public opinion that the true character of traditional song could not be made generally known. It is difficult to see how, even now, this can be otherwise, at least as far as the schools are concerned. *O No John* and *The Keeper* as printed in Novello's *School Songs* are admirable additions to the classroom repertoire, and few teachers, even now, would care to teach their children the actual words of these songs as transcribed by Sharp. Still, the wholesale expurgation of innocently wanton verses did leave a feeling of dissatisfaction, not only in Sharp's mind but in the minds of other editors. An interesting statement of this feeling was left by another collector, Alfred Williams:[2]

> Besides the legitimate pieces there were many 'rough' songs in circulation. I make no apology for them. I do not know, indeed, that any is needed. They were rude, but not altogether bad. Many of them were

---

[1] Cecil Sharp: *English Folk Songs, Some Conclusions.*
[2] Alfred Williams: *Folk-Songs of the Upper Thames* (Duckworth, 1923).

THE IDIOM OF THE PEOPLE

satirical. In fact, the most of that kind of which I have heard were so. They dealt chiefly with immorality; not to encourage or suggest it, but to satirize it. No doubt they served the purpose for which they were intended, in some cases, at any rate, though we of our time should call them indelicate. And such, to us, they certainly are. Yet the simple, unspoiled rustic folks did not consider them out of place. They saw no harm in them. But they knew not shame, as we do. They were really very innocent compared with ourselves. We have had our eyes opened, but at what a price! I have more than once, on being told an indelicate song, had great difficulty in persuading the rustic, my informant, that I could not show the piece, and therefore should not write it. 'But why not?' I have been asked. 'There was nothing wrong with that.' Neither was there, really, though the eagerly apprehensive minds of most people to-day would soon read wrong into it. The unsophisticated villagers feel hurt at the decision and often discover considerable embarrassment, though if I were to be candid, I should say that, upon such occasions, I myself have felt something of a hypocrite. Of a truth, the shame is on our side, and lies not with the rustics. And where the songs were professedly bad, this much might be said of them—they were so honestly. That is to say, they were simple, open, and natural. They were morally immoral, if I may say so, and not cunningly suggestive and damnably hypocritical, as are some of the modern music-hall pieces.

It is not to be wondered at that, during the century that had passed since the publication of Dr Thomas Bowdler's famous *Family Shakespeare* in 1818, the minds of conscientious editors should have become somewhat mixed-up. Musicians, antiquarians, folk song collectors and educational administrators had been extolling the beauty, the purity, the directness and the simplicity of the popular idiom, only to have to admit that the people were now too refined to be allowed to know it.

Nevertheless, Sharp, for one, was well aware of the potential value of his contribution to our knowledge of traditional poetry. He claimed no expert familiarity with the subject, and made no secret of his primary concern with music. But he went to great trouble to compare the words he collected with such broadside texts as were accessible. He endeavoured to extend his conclusions about the nature of folk music to cover folk poetry. Much time and ink were expended on questions of definition which now seem somewhat academic. Undoubtedly there is a fundamental distinction between 'folk' songs and 'art' or 'composed' songs—a distinc-

THE REVISION OF FOLK SONG WORDS

tion which was never very clear in the minds of any but experts, such as Sharp himself, and which has become even more blurred under American influence. Undoubtedly the expression 'folk song', as now used, has a far wider application than ever Sharp dreamed of. It would be difficult, even among scholars, to restore the distinction in its original purity, if only because the traditional product has become so inextricably entangled with other elements. We are on safer ground if we try to make a distinction between the traditional and the commercial in popular art. We can—not always, but often —*feel* the difference, even if we cannot define it, between something made for love, fun, or pleasure, and something made for money. That is the real distinction, however hard it may be to apply it in practice. Not everything made for money is without merit; but we are surely justified in thinking that the lasting value of a work of art depends on its springing, partly at least, from motives other than commercial ones. Sharp was right in his instinctive preference for songs which arose from a love of singing to those which arose from any other motive. He retained much of the idealism of early Fabian Socialism, its genuine lack of concern about money, its inherent belief in the rightness and beauty of what had been treasured and handed down among the common people. His belief in the corrupting influence of the broadsides on folk song tradition arose partly from his dislike of the commercial product. The inferiority of the broadside to the traditional ballad or song was due in part to its emanating from the towns, for the enrichment of urban printers who knew and cared little about their country customers.[1] This

---

[1] The whole question of the relations between the urban broadsides and street-songs and the traditional songs of the countryside is very complicated. It is clear that there was a two-way traffic: not only were street-songs sold and learned in the country, but traditional songs were taken down from country people by hawkers from the town printers, who thereupon issued them as ballad sheets. The following account of his activities in the country by an early nineteenth-century street vendor of broadsides throws an interesting light on the taste of the town as received in the country (Henry Mayhew: *op. cit.*):

'Then there's the Liverpool Tragedy—that's very attractive. It's a mother murdering her own son, through gold. . . . This is a deeper tragedy than the Scarborough Murder. That suits young people better; they like to hear about the young woman being seduced by the naval officer; but the mothers take more to the Liverpool Tragedy—it suits them better. . . . There's nothing beats a stunning good murder after all. . . . I've been away with the Mannings in the country ever since. I've been through Hertfordshire, Cambridgeshire,

may be so. The broadsides have merits of their own and are a form of literature distinct from the traditional songs which were mainly of rural origin. Sharp, however, was convinced that the words of folk songs had been corrupted by broadside influence in a way that the melodies had not, since the latter were rarely given on the broadsides on account of expense. At all events, the qualitative comparison of words and music is worse than profitless if it leads to the neglect and under-valuation of a body of verse which has at least some intrinsic worth and interest. How, in any case, are we to assess the quality of folk poetry without first studying it? Much of it remains, and has always remained, shut up in specialist journals and other publications of limited circulation, or in virtually inaccessible mss.

Sharp believed that in the past more attention had been paid to the words of traditional songs than to their tunes. So far as the great collections of Child and others are concerned, this is undeniably true. But now that folk music, largely through the example and work of Sharp and his predecessors, has been firmly established in the musical life of the nation, it is time once more to restore the balance. Of his own principal contribution to the theory of folk music (*Some Conclusions*) Sharp wrote:

> This book is concerned with the music of the folk-song rather than with its text. As, however, it was impossible to avoid all mention of folk-words, this chapter has been included. Much has been written about folk-poetry in general, but very little about the traditional poetry of England. It is hoped that a book on this branch of the subject will some day be written, in which scientific use will be made of the material now being amassed by collectors. No attempt is here made to forestall any such enterprise.

I take this as the blessing of a generous and single-minded scholar on a great future study of which this book is intended as a small and inadequate beginning.

---

and Suffolk, along with George Frederick Manning and his wife—travelled from 800 to 1000 miles with 'em, but I could have done much better if I'd stopped in London.'

4

THE SHARP MANUSCRIPTS

Cecil Sharp's mss. were left to Clare College, Cambridge, where they are preserved in the Forbes Library. They consist of fifty cloth and leather bound notebooks comprising the following:

WORDS	
English ballads and songs[1]	14 volumes
English carols, religious songs, chanteys and singing games	1 volume
American songs	5 volumes
MUSIC (mainly tunes, but with some words, in many cases first stanzas only)	23 volumes
FOLK DANCE NOTES	4 volumes
INDEX to English and American songs	3 volumes

The subject of the present study is the fourteen volumes of English song and ballad words, though occasional reference has been made to the other volumes of words and music, both English and American, for the purpose of comparison. There is still room for an exhaustive study of the whole collection, but for a number of reasons I believe the fourteen volumes mentioned to contain the most interesting part of Sharp's discoveries not hitherto made public. The religious songs and carols have been published with little alteration; the chanteys compare unfavourably with those collected elsewhere; the American songs have been for the most part published without alteration. They represent a part of Sharp's activities which was more or less detached from his work in England; they were late fruits of his researches, and have received wide and deserved attention. It is no part of the present study to examine these, or in any way to refer to them except in passing. I would say this, however—that in my opinion they have been allowed unjustly to overshadow the main body of Sharp's English collection. The Appalachian songs were something quite fresh in folk song discovery, Sharp being one of the first in that field, but

[1] In his publications Sharp made a loose distinction between ballads and songs—that is, broadly speaking, narrative and lyrical pieces; but the distinction seems to me to have had little significance for him, or for us.

only a late arrival among collectors in England. The notion that he brought back a fabulous horde of 'English' songs which had persisted unspoilt for centuries in the Appalachians gained wide currency; and owing to the fact that publication of these was intended for a later, adult public, whereas much of Sharp's English publishing was undertaken for Edwardian schoolchildren, a fuller and juster picture of the American discoveries was available. Some of the versions of songs which he obtained in America seem to me, by comparison with their English counterparts, confused in meaning and coarser in feeling. This is not to deny that there are many wonderful things in the Appalachian volumes; but so too are there in the English mss., and these have never previously been published as they were taken down.

Nor have I paid more than casual attention to the tunes. In the first place, I am no musician; secondly, Sharp appears to have published the best of the tunes unaltered. Miss Karpeles informs me that he never altered a melody, however much he was tempted to do so. The publication of music is a costly and relatively unprofitable business; but it is not without regret that I have been obliged to ignore the melodies, and I hope that the time will come when many of Sharp's unpublished melodies may appear in print. It is not that he altered the tunes he printed, but rather that for practical purposes he was obliged to choose one—presumably in his opinion the best—of a number of alternative tunes in the case of many well-known songs. So that such and such a tune—for instance, *O No John*—has come to be regarded as the tune for those particular words. I believe that the music volumes still contain almost untapped melodic resources.

My justification for printing words without tunes is threefold: first, it has always been done in the case of popular poetry—by the great ballad editors, for instance; secondly, the folk song collections published during the past hundred years have been essentially the work of musicians and have been concerned primarily with the dissemination of folk music as distinct from poetry; thirdly, the fact that different versions of the words of a particular song were sung by different singers to quite different tunes proves that it was the exception for a set of words to be indissolubly associated with one tune. Much of our poetic literature, traditional or 'composed', has become divorced from its original musical association—for instance, the border ballads and the lyrics of Wyatt and other Tudor

THE SHARP MANUSCRIPTS

poets. Nevertheless, this is no reason for regarding either the words or the tunes of folk songs as unimportant, or for thinking of a folk song as other than an organic whole, in which words and music play an equal part. The ideal, no doubt, is a great national collection of songs giving authentic texts of both words and tunes, with all the important variants. The scale of such an undertaking can scarcely be imagined. The present study is concerned with only a fragment of the non-musical part of the field.

There are in the Sharp collection 3,374 pages of words, of which 1,018 are the American songs. The latter are in typescript, the work of Miss Karpeles, who also was responsible for the index to the whole collection. The 2,356 pages of the English words, which have been the main field of my researches, are mostly in Sharp's handwriting. At its best this is round and legible, and certain idiosyncrasies, such as the tendency to form o's like a's, are easily allowed for. Unhappily, however, Sharp suffered from a complaint which, fifty years ago, was diagnosed as 'gout of the eyes', but which would probably now be called 'iritis'. This caused acute pain and inflammation, and sometimes made Sharp roll on the floor in agony. When he was tired, therefore, or his eyes were troubling him, his writing was far from legible, and I cannot be certain that I have transcribed every word accurately.

These fourteen volumes of English traditional verse in ms. represent a tireless and devoted labour over a long period—about seventeen years in fact, allowing for an interval of three or four years in which Sharp was occupied mainly with his American collection. I do not know what proportion of the songs he listened to in Somerset and the neighbouring counties are recorded in these notebooks. I fancy that he took down everything that he regarded as a traditional song, even if he knew it to be only the words of a well-known and not very interesting broadside; he also took down many versions, almost identical, of songs that had been noted previously by himself or other collectors. I am certain that he always took down exactly what he heard, except in very rare instances, even if he could not always make sense of it. Often the singer's memory was at fault. But how much irrelevant material he was obliged to listen to will probably never be known. Presumably, this is one of the hardships of any collector's life. So far as I can discover, he only once or twice noted the words of a composed song, though he

THE IDIOM OF THE PEOPLE

certainly had to listen patiently through many worthless music-hall and 'popular' pieces, of modern composition. Yet a great deal of what he took down, even after enforced selection, is of small interest to a student of genuine traditional poetry; the fact that he recorded so much that is poor is a proof of his pertinacity and thoroughness as a scholar, and an indication that nothing of literary value which he heard went unrecorded.

In outlining the contents of these fourteen volumes, mention must first be made of the material which I have not drawn on for the present selection. It is, I think, mainly of small value and can only interest the most omnivorous expert in one or other branch of minor verse.

First, there are versions of a good many traditional ballads already well known through earlier collections, such as those of Percy and Child. I will refer later to those which I have found sufficiently interesting to reprint—interesting, that is, as variants, not so far as I know recorded elsewhere. For the rest, Sharp noted versions of the following standard ballads, in all cases either closely parallel to the published texts, or inferior to them:

> The Bailiff's Daughter of Islington
> Barbara Allen
> The Golden Vanity[1]
> Gypsy Laddie (12 versions)
> Henry Martin
> High Barbary
> Lady Maisry
> Lambkin (3)
> Little Musgrave and Lady Barnard
> Lord Bateman
> Lord Lovel
> Lord Rendal
> Lord Thomas and Fair Elinor (4)

---

[1] Sharp's versions of *The Golden Vanity* contain the following interesting variant, but are not otherwise remarkable.
> The little boy jumped overboard and swam to her ship's side
> The one was at the cards the other at the dice
> So he took two borers in his hand he bored two holes at once
> So the water flowed so strong they couldn't work the pumps.

THE SHARP MANUSCRIPTS

The Outlandish Knight
Sir Hugh (4 English, 9 American versions)
Six Dukes
Two *Robin Hood* ballads
The Unquiet Grave (6)

The chief fact of interest here is the evidence that the standard ballads were still known, though for the most part in fragmentary, corrupt or confused form, in the West of England some centuries after the time of their origin.[1] Another point of interest is the almost total absence of the supernatural in the songs remembered by English—as distinct from Celtic or Gaelic—people. There are exceptions, but on the whole this holds true throughout the area explored by Sharp.

The bulk of the songs which he noted in England, however, were inferior broadside productions, usually on hack themes and in pedestrian doggerel. Typical in form, though exceptionally gruesome in theme, is *The Oxford Murder*, a long-winded composition in which a girl is courted by a gamekeeper and becomes pregnant. She appeals to him to marry her, but by now he is courting another girl. He stabs the first girl to death, cuts open her body and finds twins. He places them in her arms and lays the corpse in a thorn-bush. Meanwhile, having heard cries, the neighbours inform her parents, who are heart-broken; the gamekeeper is apprehended and hanged. It was, no doubt, the bulk of this sort of material that gave Sharp his rather low opinion of the words of English traditional songs; and its relative scarcity in the repertoire of Appalachian singers may have accounted in part for his enthusiasm over his American discoveries.

His mss. include a number of fragments or inferior versions of songs which have been well known for many years—for instance, *Jolly Good Ale and Old*, *The Farmer's Curst Wife*, *O Good Ale* and *The Leather Bottèl*. A number of fragments of genuine folk songs are given in the appendix at the end of this volume. Under the title *Midsummer Fair* Sharp also took down a version of *Widdecombe Fair*

---

[1] In an article in the *Journal of the English Folk Dance and Song Society* for December 1955, Marie Slocombe gives evidence for the survival, even at the present time, of many of these traditional ballads among singers in Ireland. Here the supernatural element is much more prominent.

21

THE IDIOM OF THE PEOPLE

notable only for the odd refrain which replaces the list of Devon names in the standard versions:

> To my oore hag boar, bag nigger bag a wallah and bantaballoo.

There are few comic songs of any merit; those in rural dialect, such as *The Hornet and the Bittle*, must be regarded as literary compositions. *Buttercup Joe* and *Harry the Tailor* are also too self-consciously rustic to be considered authentic. On the other hand, *Logan's Bright Water, Sweet Jenny of the Moor* and *A Sweet Country Life*[1] are examples of genteel writing adopted by country singers.

There are many uninspired political and patriotic pieces emanating from the tin-pan alley of Georgian and Regency days. There are verses about Nelson, Napoleon and Robert Emmett, as well as Maria Marten and other figures from popular melodrama. There are a few occupational songs about the regular agricultural pursuits of the ploughman, the harvester and the shepherd,[2] as well as more numerous ditties about poaching, dicing and highway robbery. There are picaresque ballads on stereotyped models and innumerable sentimental love songs probably originating in Georgian concert-rooms and Victorian music-halls, about faithful shepherdesses, devoted swains, bold tars, roving blades, venturesome servant-girls and handsome squires.[3] These are the stock characters of light opera and popular song during the eighteenth and nineteenth centuries; the artificial cliché-ridden verse in which they are celebrated is at best smooth and slick, at worst coarse and clumsy. At all times banal and monotonous, it is no better and no worse than the output of tin-pan alley any time and anywhere.

From this, the dross of centuries, emerge two streams—one of lively, vigorous traditional verse, sturdy, resourceful, direct, humorous and natural; the other, a far more slender and intermittent stream, of imaginative poetry, pure both in feeling and in expression.

[1] For these three pieces see Appendix, pp. 234–236.
[2] A somewhat garbled piece of propaganda for the wool trade is given in the Appendix, p. 241.
[3] See Appendix, p. 236.

5
THE IDIOM OF THE PEOPLE

Sharp collected in England nearly 800 different songs and ballads.[1] Of these I have transcribed for this selection 115. About forty have not, so far as I can ascertain, appeared in print before, though some may be buried in uncatalogued collections of broadsides. What is of greater interest, however, is that scarcely any have hitherto been published exactly as they were taken down, and as they appear here. The few exceptions are those which have been given verbatim in the *Journal of the Folk-Song Society*, which is not and never has been on the general market. Even those which were originally published with only slight emendations are for the most part out of print. It is now possible, therefore, for the general reader, as distinct from the student of mss., to begin to assess the scope, the interest and the value of English traditional verse.

It has seemed to me important to reprint these songs exactly as Sharp took them down—that is, as they were sung to him by the country people in the West of England during the first two decades of this century. Most of these singers were in their sixties or seventies, and for a long time many had not been called upon to remember the songs of their youth. It is obvious that their memories often failed, or brought to the surface a confused or fragmentary version of something that had once been clear and complete. Their grammar is often unconventional, and some of the sentences they sang would now be written off by the educated as simply illiterate. Malapropisms were introduced. Easy and tempting as it would have been to 'correct' these errors, to regularize syntax, emend faulty rhymes and generally render these poems consistent with literary practice, I have deliberately avoided the temptation and left them alone. I have also retained Sharp's scanty and haphazard punctuation, since even this may help the reader to approach more nearly the atmosphere in which he worked. It helps to preserve the sense of oral tradition, punctuation being essentially a literary device. Spoken or sung verses are punctuated naturally by the line-breaks,

---

[1] The figure of 2,813 English songs given in the *Life* is inclusive of variants, and also of carols, chanteys and singing games, which have been discounted for the purpose of the present study.

THE IDIOM OF THE PEOPLE

and the absence of quotation-marks for the use of direct speech and at a change of speakers compels the close attention which verse demands. Once the reader has become accustomed to the lack of punctuation, I think it will increase his sense of closeness to the original singers.

Exceptions to the rule of exact transcription are these: I have occasionally made an obvious emendation where failure to do so would hinder understanding. I have sometimes adopted a reading from another version noted by Sharp, in order to help the meaning. In all such cases the alteration is indicated in the textual notes. I have also standardized the use of the apostrophe in abbreviations such as *I'm* and *won't*.

It has been my practice as a rule to print the most complete version in the mss., with additions or variants from other versions mentioned in the notes. In some dozen cases the existence of a number of versions of equal merit and completeness, or incompleteness, has created a problem. I have felt obliged to solve this by giving composite texts consisting of lines and stanzas from two or more versions. I have in no case resorted to this without stating it in the notes, nor have I introduced anything not found in Sharp's mss. The alternatives were either to give a less complete text than was available, or to print all the versions[1] and leave the reader to make his choice. The latter could not be done generally without much repetition and waste of space. Thus, while I have in every case tried to give a readable version, it has been no part of my intention to 'restore' a hypothetical original or establish a received text. The time for that will come, if ever, only after a great deal more work has been done in publishing and collating all the available mss. and texts. So much remodelling of folk song words has been done in the past, so much re-writing, abridging, emending, that it seems to me time to take steps in the opposite direction and have a look at the actual words as they left the singers' lips fifty years ago.

The literary 'faults' of folk poetry, its inconsistencies, its ignorance of some of the taboos of polite intercourse, as well as its verbal variation, and what might be called its fluidity as between one locality and another, one singer and another, one period and another —all this is inseparable from its peculiar virtues and attractions, and

[1] One song, *The Foggy Dew*, has been chosen for treatment in this way, and may be studied on pp. 45–57 of this Introduction.

THE IDIOM OF THE PEOPLE

cannot be eliminated without loss to its unique character. Inevitably, when we commit an oral tradition to print, we kill something. A printed collection of ballads is necessarily something of a literary museum. It is in order to keep these examples of the idiom of the people as fresh and organic as possible that they are here presented with the minimum of editing.

The poems in this selection are few in relation to the whole body of folk poetry, but they are sufficient to show the range and variety which it embraces. We are accustomed to think of such ballads as *The Wife of Usher's Well* as belonging to a remote past, and textually 'fixed' by editors such as Child and his predecessors. But Sharp collected two versions of it which show that the ballad was still organic in oral tradition long after it had been written and printed. *Lord Thomas of Winesbury*, *The Banks of Green Willow* and several others are versions of ballads in Child's collection. *Blow away the Morning Dew* is a partly narrative, partly lyrical song derived from another Child ballad, *The Baffled Knight*. There is also a good version of *The Broomfield Wager*. *Still Growing*, *Three Maids a Rushing* and *Young* Barnswell are ballads which do not appear in Child.

For reasons indicated in the notes, several songs in this selection appear to be medieval survivals or to contain traces of medieval minstrelsy—for example, *Maid freed from the Gallows*, *The Keeper*, and *Gently Johnny my Jingalo*. A hitherto unpublished fragment, *I sowed some Seeds*, also seems to be of pre-Elizabethan origin. The same may be said of *Jolly Old Hawk*, which is evidently the remains of a song sung to accompany a game. There are other survivals of riddles, cumulative songs, and songs connected with children's games, such as *Pery Mery Dixi Domine*, *The Tree in the Wood* and *As I was going to Banbury*.

While there are few undeniably comic songs of ancient origin, the comic spirit is prevalent in many, such as *Whistle Daughter Whistle* and *Gossip Joan*; while the element of satirical exaggeration is clearly marked in *The Derby Ram*. The latter is connected with a piece of traditional ritual drama, just as *Poor Old Horse* was also at one time the accompaniment to a mummers' performance.

The supernatural, as Sharp and other English collectors noticed, is conspicuously absent. Whether this is an Anglo-Saxon attitude, or whether it is the result of a gradual process of rationalization, is not clear. Certainly songs about witches were rare in the south of England by the nineteenth century, but in *Hares on the Mountains* there is certainly a reference to magical powers of transformation. This is one of the many songs concerned with courtship, of which two of the best are *O No John* and *Ripest Apples*. *Keys of Heaven* has some kinship with these and, like *Three Maids a Milking*, makes free use of symbolism.

When Feste asks Sir Toby and Sir Andrew whether they want a love song or a song of good life, they reply enthusiastically, 'A love-song, a love-song', and their preference is echoed throughout popular tradition. The great majority of the best of Sharp's songs are concerned, directly or indirectly, with courtship. The mutual attraction of the sexes, its progress and effects, was the central theme celebrated, during the years of its greatest vigour, in the oral tradition of the English countryside. To some the constant recurrence of the theme may seem monotonous, but the ways in which it is handled are of infinite variety.[1] A strongly pagan, amoral outlook pervades the treatment of the theme. At least ten of the courtship songs in this selection are connected, even if only vestigially, with the ancient rites which accompanied May Day and Midsummer. It is no empty formula that begins so many folk songs—'As I walked out one May morning' or 'one Midsummer morn'. I am inclined to think that in England these two festivals, much more clearly differentiated in Mediterranean countries, became confused in the popular mind. It may be that much that was elsewhere associated with May Day was put off till Midsummer because of the uncertainty of the northern climate. Whether or not this is so, both

---

[1] In *English Folk Song: Some Conclusions* Sharp commented as follows on the prevalence of love songs:

In point of time the song succeeded the ballad, of which, in a sense, it is the lineal descendant. 'Love' is the perennial theme of the folk-singer of all lands. The English peasant is no exception to this rule, and a very large proportion of his songs are love-songs. These are not, however, of the intense, erotic type which is so common among the southern nations of Europe. The Englishman's love-song is of the adventurous, open air order, with love at first sight, hastily reciprocated, to the accompaniment of nightingales and the breaking into blossom of buds at springtime. 'As I went out one May morning', is the motto which might be affixed to the majority of them. It is the Englishman's way to look on the bright side of things, to view life from the standpoint of May rather than of December.

THE IDIOM OF THE PEOPLE

A Maypole Dance: Woodcut of the time of Charles I

occasions were, in pre-Puritan England, marked by celebrations which sometimes became orgiastic, and which the Church tried always to control or suppress. The Calvinistic Philip Stubbes wrote thus of the May Day festivities:

> Against Maie, Whitsondaie, or some other tyme of the yeare, every parishe, towne, and village, assemble themselves together, both the men, women and children, olde and yong, even all indifferently; and either goyng all together or dividyng themselves into companies, they goe some to the woodes and groves, some to the hilles and mountaines, some to one place, some to an other, where they spende all the night in pleasant pastymes, and in the mornyng they returne, bringing with them birch, bowes and braunches of trees, to deck their assemblies withall. And no marvaile, for there is a great lord present amongest them, as super-intendent and lorde over their pastymes and Sportes, namely, Sathan, prince of hell. But their cheefest iewell they bring from thence is their Maie poole, whiche they bring home with greate veneration, as thus: they have twentie or fortie yoke of oxen, every oxe havyng a sweete nosegaie of flowers tyed on the tippe of his hornes, and these oxen drawe home this Maie poole (this stinkyng idoll rather), which is covered all over

THE IDIOM OF THE PEOPLE

with flowers and hearbes, bounde rounde aboute with stringes, from the top to the bottome, and sometyme painted with variable colours, with twoo or three hundred men, women, and children followyng it with greate devotion. And thus beying reared up, with handkercheifes and flagges streamyng on the toppe, they strawe the ground aboute, binde greene boughes about it, sett up sommer haules, bowers, and arbours hard by it; and then fall they to banquet and feast, to leape and daunce aboute it, as the heathen people did at the dedication of their idolles, whereof this is a perfect patterne, or rather the thing it self. I have heard it credibly reported (*and that viva voce*) by men of great gravitie, credite, and reputation, that of fortie, three score, or a hundred maides goyng to the woode over night, there have scarcely the third parte of them returned home againe undefiled.[1]

Of dancing we are told:

> Dauncing, as it is used (or rather abused) in these daies, is an introduction to whordome, a preparative to wantonnesse, a provocative to uncleannesse, and an introite to all kinde of lewdnesse, rather then a pleasant exercise to the mind, or a wholesome practise for the bodie (as some list to call it).[1]

And of vagrant ballad-singers:

> I thinke that all good minstrelles, sober and chast musitions (speaking of suche dronken sockettes, and baudie parasites as raunge the countries, rimyng and singyng of uncleane, corrupte, and filthie songes, in tavernes, ale-houses, innes, and other publique assemblies), maie daunce the wilde Moris through a needle's eye. For how should they beare chaste mindes, seeyng that their exercise is the pathwaie to all uncleannesse? There is no ship so balanced with massie matter as their heades are fraught with all kinde of baudie songes, filthie ballades, and scurvie rimes, serving for every purpose and for every companie.[1]

In this way Stubbes and other Puritan writers inveighed also against Whitsun ales, gay clothing, plays, wakes, bear-baitings and all other manifestations of diabolical influence. But writers and clergymen of the old school looked back later with affection upon these survivals of pagan England. Herrick's address to Corinna, and his other celebrations of country customs and ritual, show that the country way of life in England was firmly established. What was lost perhaps by the Puritan revolution was the unconscious innocence of amorality, the natural sensuality of healthy and youthful love.

[1] Philip Stubbes: *The Anatomie of Abuses* (1585).

THE IDIOM OF THE PEOPLE

What the Puritans substituted was a sort of sensuality of repression.

The best of the love songs in oral tradition are pre-Puritan in spirit, if not in date. *Blow away the Morning Dew, I'm Seventeen Come Sunday* and *The Foggy Dew* can joke about sex in a way impossible in sophisticated verse after the sixteenth century. *Long and Wishing Eye* and *Searching for Lambs* express a Theocritean combination of robust sensuality and joyful tenderness which is hard to find elsewhere. *As I walked through the Meadows* and *The Lark in the Morn* are in the same vein, and bowdlerization can only transform them into another sort of song altogether.

A related theme is that of the girl betrayed by her lover. In some of the best of all traditional poems it is treated tragically—for instance, in *Waly Waly and The Seeds of Love*. More often it is treated in the spirit of comedy, with philosophical worldliness. The implication of such songs as *The Bold Grenadier* and *Cold Blow and a Rainy Night* is that a girl seduced and deserted by a soldier gets no more than she deserves. Again, the theme of enforced separation is treated in a variety of ways—with the intensity of tragic despair in *The Turtle Dove,* with stoicism in *High Germany,* and with humour in *The Rout of the Blues.*

In these love songs, apart from some crudities and some expressions of callousness, we hear the idiom of the people at its best and most characteristic. We hear, in Keats's expressive phrase, 'the voice of true feeling'. The sense of tragedy never degenerates into morbidity, the sense of delight remains rooted in sensuality and never becomes sentimental. It lacks the intellectual intensity of more sophisticated love poetry, but it has something difficult to find in literary poetry after, say, Donne—a quality well described by Herrick as 'cleanly wantonness'. There is nothing rarefied about it; it reveals the hearts of ordinary men and women.

Just as there are songs of too credulous girls betrayed, so there are others which tell of. clever girls who win husbands by strategy. *An Alderman's Lady, Mowing the Barley* and *Poor Nell* are among these. In the latter two the listener has the added pleasure of seeing a lawyer outwitted. These belong to the street-song tradition of town-made pieces, not the rural tradition of the songs of love and courtship and separation.

If courtship is treated now light-heartedly, now romantically, marriage is almost always a subject for satire. In some of the courting songs it is assumed, that marriage is a desirable outcome, but very few songs treat of marriage itself as more than just tolerable. In many it is regarded as an unqualified disaster. *Single Men's Warning* and *On Monday Morning I Married a Wife* are typical. On the other hand *Good Old Man* displays a sense of solid matrimonial affection, and in *The Sign of the Bonny Blue Bell* a girl speaks of marriage with whole-hearted approval. There are, too, examples of farcical courting and marriage songs like *Arthur Bradley O* and *When shall we get Married.*

A good many songs have an occupational character, and bear witness to the wholeness and variety of the oral tradition by showing how its verse touches upon all the members of a rural community. *Joan's Ale was New* contains a catalogue of tradesmen, *The Tailor by his Trade*, *The Roving Journeyman* and *The Miller and the Lass* are further examples. *Bold Robinson* deals with pugilism, *Poaching Song* and *Sheep Stealer* with illegal occupations. A considerable number of songs treat of soldiers and sailors not only as the downfall of foolish girls but also as upholders of the national honour.

In so far as any generalizations about such varied material are valid, it seems that true folk songs are the result of oral tradition in a rural society; the love songs which have been discussed above are, in many instances, the lyrical or emotional element in ballads, probably detached from their original narrative context and expanded into complete, self-sufficient poems, sometimes with the addition of a refrain. Other themes are added to the rural singer's repertoire through the medium of the printed broadside, emanating from the towns. It is often possible to distinguish the urban product by its greater smartness and wit, as distinct from the simplicity and emotional sincerity of the country folk song. It has a commercial flavour entirely lacking in the traditional song. Most of the pieces about crime seem to have originated from the towns. *Adieu to Old England* and *Van Dieman's Land* are broadside ballads about transportation. *Jack Hall* and *The Rambling Boy* are about thieves, and *The Two Butchers* describes a very unsavoury kind of highway robbery. There is little if any tendency to glamorize the criminal. The romantic highwayman seems to be entirely a creation of quite modern fiction.

Throughout Sharp's mss. there is a fair sprinkling of 'merrytales', usually on the theme of cuckoldry. Many of these were probably

THE IDIOM OF THE PEOPLE

merrier at the time of their composition than they are to our ears. But a few of the more vigorous and ingenious examples have been included. The cuckold has always been regarded as a figure of fun, though sometimes he is treated sympathetically, while the seducer is ridiculed. There is a kind of gusto, a generosity of outlook, about *The Sea Captain* which gives distinction to a thoroughly disreputable story.

The folk songs noted by collectors at the turn of the last century do no doubt reveal a culture in decline, a community afflicted by prolonged agricultural depression and the continual drain of its most vigorous members into the towns. Yet the collective memory was still strong amongst the older country people, and that memory was enriched by its inheritance from a great and flourishing past, when England had been predominantly agricultural. The poetic and musical inheritance was far from homogeneous: it contained ballads four centuries old, side by side with the street-songs of Victorian peddlers, medieval lyric fragments of perhaps Norman-French origin, seventeenth-and eighteenth-century broadsides and tavern songs, and the products of Georgian concert-rooms and pleasure-gardens. Yet the collective mind assimilated everything, adding much and discarding much, exercising a selective instinct in retaining what it felt it could make its own. In choosing from the mass of available material, I have taken what seems to me most vigorous, most direct, most economical in language, most imaginative in expression, and most truly and deeply felt. This traditional verse is unique and valuable because it is lively, energetic, concrete, idiomatic, rhythmically vital, natural, without meretricious artifice, and capable at times of amazingly imaginative utterance. In Keats's phrase, it can Surprise by a fine excess'. At its most intense it seems to draw upon a fund of imagery which belongs not to the mind of a single poet but to the hidden emotional life of all who speak and know English. There is much that is humdrum, pedestrian, clumsily expressed; but in this respect it is the reflection of the lives of ordinary people, in which, too, there is something that soars, and moves, and stirs. Consider:

> There's not a swish goes round my waist
> Nor a comb goes in my hair
> Neither fire light nor candle light
> Can ease my heart's despair

THE IDIOM OF THE PEOPLE

and

    There's many a one so bad as he and why should I complain
    For love it is a killing thing did you ever feel the pain?

and

        Did she lay so close to you Billy Boy
          Billy Boy
        Did she lay so close to you Billy Boy?
        Yes she lay so close to me
        As the rind unto the tree
        She's my Nancy, please-my-fancy
        I'm her charming Billy Boy

and

        When I wore my apron low
        My love followed me through frost and snow
        When I wore it up to my chin
        My love passed by and never looked in

and

        There is a man on yonder hill
        He's got two hearts like iron and steel

and

        I had two dogs under my father's table
        They do prick their ears when they do hear the horn

and

        The crow that is so black my dear
        Shall change his colour white
        If ever I prove false to thee
        The day shall turn to night my dear
        The day shall turn to night

and

        I sowed some seed all in some grove
        All in some grove there grows no green

and

        Yesterday in the morning gray
        Parted poor Tom and I
        I heard a bird singing in the wood
        Poor Tom was like to die.

6
SOME FOLK SONGS CONSIDERED

The rest of these introductory pages are devoted to a more detailed consideration of certain topics which so far have only been touched on. In particular, five of the songs in this selection have been chosen for analysis, since they seem to me to be of special interest in considering these matters.

First, by what process is a folk song transformed into an art song, and reconditioned to suit the taste of an age of refinement? By what process can it be restored to something more nearly approaching its original state? In answering these questions, I have taken *O No John* for the purpose of illustration.

Secondly, what is the relation between ballads and folk songs? By what changes is the one transformed into the other? A few pages earlier it was suggested that many folk songs are 'the lyrical or emotional element in ballads, probably detached from their original narrative context and expanded into complete, self-sufficient poems, sometimes with the addition of a refrain'. In this connection, detailed reference is made to *Waly Waly* and *Blow away the Morning Dew*.

Thirdly, there is an analysis of *A Brisk Young Lover*, in order to illustrate the multiplicity and variety of the different versions of a single song as it has evolved among different groups of singers.

Lastly, there is an examination and comparison of several versions of *The Foggy Dew*, in an attempt to arrive at an understanding of a song whose meaning has been obscured by time and corruption, even though its popularity has not been extinguished.

O NO JOHN (No. 68)

Between 1903 and 1908 Sharp collected four versions of the song known as *O No John*. This was published in the form known to everyone in *Folk Songs from Somerset*, 1904-9, in Novello's *School*

THE IDIOM OF THE PEOPLE

Songs, 1908, and again in *English Folk Songs*, Selected. Edition, 1921, Vol. II. Sharp's note in the latter volume is as follows: 'The first two stanzas of the text are exactly as they were sung to me; the rest of the lines were coarse and needed considerable revision.' In fact the words were so completely re-written as to make a new song, in which there is no seduction but a pretty romance concluding with wedding-bells. The melody, on the other hand, is exactly as taken down from one of the singers. (It is a good tune, and justly popular; but it may be of interest to point out that what has become *the* tune of *O No John* is only one of several, and that at least one or two of the others are of some musical worth.) In this form the song has been sung all over the world, in classroom and concert-hall, at home and on the radio; Mr Paul Robeson, who gained an international reputation as a singer of negro spirituals, made a gramophone record of it; and, as I write, a Soviet Russian Army choir on a visit to this country perform it as part of their repertoire. It has, in short, become a national song. Can it be said, then, that Sharp's ambition of replacing the old 'national' songs by the real traditional folk songs has, in this instance, been realized? So far as the melody is concerned, yes. But what of the words?

No other editor seems to have printed this song, though its near relations, *The Keys of Heaven* (No. 54), *My Man John, Twenty Eighteen* and *Ripest Apples* (No. 69) have been frequently noted and published in one form or another. In printing for the first time the song which Sharp collected, I have thought it best to give a composite text (No. 68) consisting of stanzas and lines from all the four ms. versions. No one version is complete by itself, but all contain interesting variants. There is no question of 'restoring' a lost 'original'; that is in all probability by now impossible. But it seems worth while to give the completest text compatible with respect for the words of the singers. This is a practice I have carried out sparingly, preferring as a rule to print a whole version together with variants from others where necessary. It seems to me more desirable on the whole to print a set of words once actually sung by someone than a 'better' set reconstructed by scholarship. It may be of interest to show how this has been done in this one instance of *O No John*. Here are the four versions as they appear in Sharp's ms: the lines which I have taken for my text are numbered and italicized.

O NO JOHN

Stanza and line numbers in composite text (No. 68)

Version A

[1285 William Morley at Bincombe 1907]

1.1	*On yonder hill there stands a creature*
1.2	*Who she is I do not know*
1.3	*I'll go and cour her for her beauty*
1.4 Refrain	*She must answer Yes or No,*
	O No John, No John, No John No.
2.1	*On her bosom are bunches of posies*
2.2	*On her breast where flowers grow*
2.3	*If I should chance to touch that posy*
2.4	*She must answer Yes or No*
	My husband was but a Spanish Captain
4.2	*Went to sea but a month ago*
4.3	*And the very last time we kissed and parted*
4.4	*He always bid me answer No,*
	One night they went to bed together
	There they lay till the cocks did crow
	Then they sport till the daylight was breaking
	Now it's time for us to go.
6.1	*Madam shall I tie your garter*
6.2	*Tie it a little above your knee*
6.3	*If my hand should slip a little farther*
6.4	*Would you think it amiss of me?*

Version B

[8 Lucy White and Louie Hooper at Hambridge 1903]
(see Plate I, facing p. 36)

My father was a Spanish Captain
Leave me to mourn five years ago
First he kist me, then he leave me
Always told me to answer No!
No Sir, No Sir, No, Sir, No!

5.1	*Madam in your face is beauty*
5.2	*In you flowers grow*[1]

[1] *you flowers* = *your bosom flowers* in text.

THE IDIOM OF THE PEOPLE

5.3 *In your bedroom there is pleasure*
5.4 *Shall I view it, yes or no?*
No Sir etc.

Madam shall I tie your garter
Shall I tie it above yr. knee?
If I should be little bolder
Would you think it rude of me?
No Sir etc.

Version C

[1777 James Beale (72) at Wareham, Kent 1908]

On yonder's hill there lives a maiden
Who she is I do not know
But I'll go and court her for her beauty
Whether she answers me yes or no
No John No, No John, No John, No John, No.

3.1 *Madam I am come for to court you*
3.2 *Whether your passions I can gain*
3.3 *Come and set yourself down alongside of me*
3.4 *Fear I should never see you again*
No John etc.

Madam may I tie up your garter
May I tie it above your knee
And if by chance my hand should slip a little farther
Should you think it amiss of me?
No John etc.

Madam and I went to bed together
Then we lied till the cocks did crow
I rifled her charm and quit her chamber
Still she answered it was no.
No John etc.

4.1 *My husband he was a Spanish Captain*
He went to sea about three months ago
And the very last time we kissed and parted
He always told me to answer no.
No John etc.

No. Sir!

My father was a Spanish Captain
Leave me to mourn five years ago
First he kest me then he leave me
Always told me to answer No!
    No Sir, no Sir, No, Sir, No!

Madam in your face is beauty
In your flowers grow
In your bedroom there is pleasure
Shall I view it, yes or no?
    No Sir etc

Madam shall I tie your garter
Shall I tie it above the knee?
If I should be little bolder
Would you think it rude of me?
    No Sir etc

Lucy White & Louie Hooper, Hambridge Dec. 23. 1903
(53)

PLATE I   A VERSION OF O NO JOHN (No. 68)
Facsimile from the Cecil Sharp Mss

> The bells shall ring mournful
> O for my dearest Polly
> And she shall be buried
> For the sake of her money.   373)
>
> Elizabeth Mogg. Aug 30" 1904

Waly Waly

> The water is wide I cant get over
> Neither have I got wings to fly
> Go & get me O some little little boat
> To carry over my true love and I
>
> Love is handsome Love is pretty
> Love is charming when its true
> As it grows older it grows colder
> And fades away like the morning dew
>
> I had two dogs under my father's table
> They do prick their ears when they do hear the horn
> When I'm dead dear it will be all over
> and I hope my friends will bury me.   374)
>
> Elizabeth Mogg. Aug 30" 1904.

PLATE 2 A VERSION OF *WALY WALY* (No. 108)
Facsimile from the Cecil Sharp Mss

O NO JOHN

Version D

[1457 Alfred Emery (78) at Othery 1908]

Madam shall I tie your garter
Tie it a little above your knee
Suppose my hand should slip a little farther
Wouldn't you think it rude of me?
No Sir No, No Sir No.
Still the fair maid answered No

7.1	*My love and I we went to bed together*
7.2	*There we lay till the cocks did crow*
7.3	*Unclose your arms my dearest jewel*
7.4	*Unclose your arms and let me go*
	No Sir etc.

It will have been noticed that, in spite of a fairly strong narrative thread, *O No John* is one of the songs in which the different singers vary considerably as to the order of the stanzas. It appears that they set little store by a fixed and logical order, though of course it must be remembered that they were mostly septuagenarians.

Elements from *O No John* have become confused with *The Keys of Heaven, My Man John* and *Ripest Apples,* but it is clear that they are distinct and separate songs, though related. *The Keys of Heaven* and *My Man John* are straightforward courtship songs; the latter is in dialogue form and introduces the helpful serving-man. *O No John* deals with a seduction involving adultery. In *Ripest Apples,* of which fuller versions are given by other collectors, the basic situation is that of a rich man courting a girl who has been in love with a handsome young man who has jilted her. Her suitor persuades her that beauty and passion are ephemeral, and worldly wisdom prevails. This is apparent from a version given in the *Journal of the Folk-Song Society,* No. 17, 1913, p. 297, but Sharp's version is less complete. *Ripest Apples* is the same song as the well-known *Twenty Eighteen,* noted by Lucy Broadwood (*English County Songs,* 1893) and others, of which Sharp noted no version. This takes its title from the refrain, which is connected with a counting or ring game.

THE IDIOM OF THE PEOPLE

WALY WALY (No. 108)

An example of the connection between ballads and folk song is provided by the well-known *Waly Waly* (No. 108). The word 'Waly' is probably a Scottish exclamation of grief equivalent to 'Woe'. The title of the song, as popularized by Sharp, indicates its very tenuous connection with a ballad 'original', though the words 'Waly waly' do not actually occur in the song.

Sharp first noted a recognizable version of the song from Mrs Caroline Cox in 1905. He took down a better version from James Thomas in 1906. He had previously collected a three-stanza song from Elizabeth Mogg in 1904 (see Plate 2, facing p. 37). This contains only one stanza—the second—connected with *Waly Waly*, a fact indisputably proved by its occurrence in the Scottish song *O Waly Waly up the Bank*, Indeed, it must have been this which led Sharp to head the ms. text *Waly Waly*. He first published it in *Folk Songs from Somerset*, III, 1906, in Novello's *School Songs*, 1908, and with a slightly fuller set of words in *English Folk Songs,* Selected Edition, 1921, Vol. I. This text consists of eight stanzas, which (apart from minor editorial modifications) are the same as those given in the present selection (p. 218), together with an opening stanza which I have not included. It is not clear why he included this 'boat' stanza (the eighth on p. 219). It is agreeable and evocative but obviously belongs to a different narrative context. Sharp's only source for this was Elizabeth Mogg, who was erratic as to what elements she associated together. In 1906 he noted the same song from this singer giving two of her original three stanzas and two fresh ones. This second Mogg version is an interesting collection of folk song elements: the original 'boat' stanza, two stanzas from some convivial song with a male protagonist, and a defective ballad stanza beginning with a superb couplet whose origin I have not been able to trace:

> I had two dogs under my father's table
> They do prick their Ears when they do hear the horn.

Sharp's published text of *Waly Waly* consists of a number of disparate elements of great intrinsic beauty, but haphazardly arranged. The arrangement I have made gives what appears to be the most logical order consistent with the juxtapositions of stanzas in the ms. versions, after the extraneous material has been excluded.

WALY WALY

Stanzas 1 and 2 are found together in that sequence in the Thomas version (989), and 3, 4 and 5 in Cox (604). Thomas lacks 3 and 4, but has 5 immediately following 2. The position of 6, found only in the first Mogg version, is established by reference to *O Waly Waly up the Bank*, My final stanza (7) is also the conclusion of the Thomas version, where it appears most logically. (This analysis may be checked by reference to the text and notes, pp. 218–220.)

Even now, however, I cannot feel that we necessarily have the words of *Waly Waly* complete. The narrative thread seems to me more elusive than is usual. The occasion of the emotional utterance is no more than hinted at. (Even *The Seeds of Love,* another song of this type, is more specific.)

In other cases of this kind we can seek help from outside sources, but here Sharp's mss. provide the fullest evidence available. Apart from Sharp, the only collectors of *Waly Waly* appear to have been Baring-Gould (*Songs of the West,* 1890) and Hammond (*Journal of the Folk-Song Society,* No. 27, 1923, collected 1905); the former in Cornwall and Devon, the latter in Dorset. Baring-Gould's text is confused and extensively re-written. It consists essentially of the 5th, 4th, 1st and 3rd stanzas of my text, interspersed with two further stanzas, one from *The Trees they do Grow High,* and the other partly from *Died of Love* and partly from *O Waly Waly up the Bank*. Hammond's text consists of the 7th, 4th and 3rd stanzas of my text, distributed among seven other stanzas, two of them from *A Brisk Young Lover,* and the other five apparently from unidentified ballad sources. Thus neither of these versions helps to clear up the confusion.

A further, and earlier, source to which we can refer is the song *O Waly Waly up the Bank,* already mentioned. Baring-Gould pointed out that two of his stanzas occur in this song; Sharp went further, and asserted that his *Waly Waly* and O *Waly Waly up the Bank* were 'closely allied' (*English Folk Songs,* Selected Edition, 1921, Vol. I: note). The fact is, however, that of his version only two stanzas, the 'oak' and the 'fading dew' (4 and 6), occur there. It has nothing else in common, except the general mood of lamentation for lost love.

O Waly Waly up the Bank contains ten stanzas in all, and is given in Percy's *Reliques* and other collections. It has a much stronger narrative thread than Sharp's *Waly Waly,* and is closely related to the ballad of *Lord Jamie Douglas*. Sidgwick (*Popular Ballads of the Olden Time*, III, 1906) described *O Waly Waly up the Bank* as 'closely interwoven' with the same ballad. Other editors went so far as to say that the song was substantially a part of the ballad.

Lord Jamie Douglas concerns the fate of Lady Barbara Erskine, daughter of the 9th Earl of Mar, who was married to the 2nd Marquis of Douglas in 1670. Told in the person of Lady Barbara, it relates how she is falsely accused by Lowrie, laird of Blackwood, of adultery with Jamie Lockhart, and, despite her pitiful entreaties, rejected by her husband. According to Child, the printed versions of this ballad usually incorporated some stanzas of the song, which was first printed fifty years before any of them.

To sum up, it seems that there was in existence during the seventeenth century—and how long before we do not know—the lament of a slighted woman, lyrical in character, but possibly with some narrative strain. About the end of the seventeenth century the woman became popularly identified with Lady Barbara Erskine, and the lament was partially incorporated in the Scottish *Lord Jamie Douglas* ballad. Either the lyrical stanzas became once more dissociated from the ballad, and gathered around themselves other elements of the same emotional character; or the original lament pursued an independent existence. In either case it subsequently emerged in the West of England, in the confused and even fragmentary forms handed down to modern folk singers. By this time there was scarcely any pretension to coherence, and quite irrelevant material had accrued to it from the traditional stock. The only quality which much of this material had in common was a general concern with various aspects of despair in love.

BLOW AWAY THE MORNING DEW (No. 14)

Percy printed a ballad called *The Baffled Knight, or Lady's Policy*. It had appeared in previous collections in various forms, and Ritson said 'Bp. Percy found the subject worthy of his best improvements.' Here is a specimen of the style of Percy's text at its most stilted:

> The lady blushed scarlet red,
>   And trembled at the stranger:
> How shall I guard my maidenhead
>   From this approaching danger?

BLOW AWAY THE MORNING DEW

> He from his saddle down did light,
> In all his riche attyer;
> And cryed, As I am a noble knight,
> I do thy charms admyer.

The ballad recounts four attempts by a foolish knight to seduce a lady, who each time outwits him. The various songs collected by Sharp confine themselves to the first attempt. According to Child, Percy's text was an abridgement of a broadside copy. Child himself used the earlier texts of Ravenscroft and Durfey, and has the refrain

> Then she sang downe a downe, hey downe deny (*bis*).

Percy has no refrain. Sidgwick (1904) printed a similar text to Child's, adding that the same theme occurs in ballads from most western European countries. Bell (1857) calls his version *Blow the Winds, I-ho!* and says it is reprinted from a broadside. The language of Bell's text shows signs of having been adapted to the Victorian view of propriety. He says it is a Northumbrian ballad', and gives as a refrain

> And blow the winds, I-ho!
> Sing, blow the winds, I-ho!
> Clear away the morning dew,
> And blow the winds, I-ho!

This he describes as 'a form common to many ballads and songs, but only to those of great antiquity.... "Io!" was an ancient form of acclamation or triumph on joyful occasions and anniversaries.' Compare Spenser, *Epithalamion*, 1.140:

> Hymen io Hymen, Hymen they do shout.

An American ballad contains an interesting development in the refrain:

> Blow the winds of morning,
> Blow the winds of Ohio.

Between 1903 and 1908 Sharp collected twelve versions which in his ms. are entitled variously *Blow away the Morning Dew*, *The Baffled Knight* and *The New Mown Hay*. Some of these contain all the elements of the story, others are fragmentary. No one version is of obvious superiority, so that I have printed two composite versions

THE IDIOM OF THE PEOPLE

A and B, and a third version *verbatim*, C. The latter, with its delightfully incongruous refrain, is possibly a marine adaptation. A and B are attempts to combine the most vigorous and coherent stanzas of two sets of parallel versions. The sources are given below each, and no extraneous words or lines are interpolated. *Folk Songs from Somerset* (1st Series, 1906) contains a genteel text in which the maiden is discovered *'beside* the watery brook', not in it.

> Cast over me my mantel fair
> And pin it o'er my gown;
> And, if you will, take hold my hand,
> And I will be your own.

The shepherd is then offered 'a kiss' and twenty thousand pounds, but nothing is said about her maidenhead, or about the cock who would not tread the hens. Sharp's note to this text says: It has been necessary for Mr Marson to soften the words.' Sharp's definitive text of this song, published in 1921, long after the association with his first collaborator, the Rev. C. L. Marson, was broken, is unchanged. He also printed three less 'softened' texts in the *Journal of the Folk-Song Society*, No. 6, 1906.

One of the interesting features in the different versions of this song is the lively variation in the form of the refrain. I have given three variants; others ring the changes on 'roll' and 'Stroll'—for example:

> Roll me in the morning, the dew and the dew
> Steal away the morning dew how sweet the winds do blow
>
> (494)

> Stroll away the morning dew
> Blow the wind I-ho.
> Stroll away the morning dew
> How sweet the winds do blow
>
> (1783)

> Hey the dewy morning
> Blow the winds heigh ho!
> Strolling in the morning dew
> How sweet the winds do blow
>
> (235)

A BRISK YOUNG LOVER

For the significance of 'marigold' (in effect, if not by derivation, the same as 'merry girl') compare Herrick, *Hesperides:*

> Give way, and be ye ravisht by the Sun,
> (And hang the head when as the Act is done)
> Spread as He spreads; wax lesse as He do's wane;
> And as He shuts, close up to Maids again.

A BRISK YOUNG LOVER (No. 20)

One of the best examples of variety and multiplicity in the proliferation of folk songs from a hypothetical common stock is that which I have given under the title *A Brisk Young Lover*. Under this title, Sharp noted eight English and four American versions; under the title *Sheffield Park* three, and under *In Castle Park* one. Other collectors printed versions under the following titles: *Died for* (or *of*) *Love, In Jessie's City, A Bold Young Farmer, There is an Alehouse in Yonder Town, A Brisk Young Sailor, I wish my baby it was born,* and *There was three worms on yonder hill*. Other songs at first sight quite different are also related, more or less distantly. It was in order to clear up this sort of confusion that Margaret Dean-Smith compiled *A Guide to English Folk Song Collections*.

Of this song Miss Dean-Smith writes: '"Died of Love" is the stock from which many fragmentations treated as separate songs have been made, including the modern burlesque "There is a tavern in the town".' There is of course no especial reason for regarding any particular song published as *Died of Love* as 'the common stock'; all we can say is that the hypothetical original dealt with a situation more or less indicated by this title, and generally implied, if only in part, in all the various versions. All contain common elements and what might be called a common mood or tone. But no version is markedly superior to the rest, nor can claim to be nearer the 'original'. It seems probable that behind this song is a lost ballad of some length and that in the various versions the original narrative elements have been to a greater or lesser degree suppressed in favour of the personal, lyrical aspects. In some versions, for instance, the only character in the song is the girl herself, the young man does not appear in person, and the mistress or mother is entirely absent. Only in one of the American versions is the moral drawn that the girl ought to have heeded her mother's advice; elsewhere the tragedy is allowed to speak for itself, and the song is concerned above all, as in most of the best folk songs, with the expression of feeling.

Any attempt at this date to reconstruct the 'original' would be purely theoretical; it seems reasonable, however, to combine the common elements into a readable text which would be fuller, less fragmentary, than any single version. From his mss. Sharp selected six stanzas which he published in *English Folk Songs*, Selected Edition, 1921, Vol. II, as *A Brisk Young Sailor*. The composite text I have printed contains seventeen stanzas, and omits none of the elements in Sharp's twelve English versions. Full as this composite text is, however, it does not contain all the elements noted by other collectors, nor would it be possible to make a satisfactory synthesis which includes *every* element. In some versions the maid-mistress relation is replaced by a daughter-parent relation. In one the father appears as 'a noble knight', and in another he discovers that his daughter has hanged herself.

> Her father he came home at night
> Saying 'Where has my daughter gone?'
> He went upstairs, the door he broke,
> And found her hanging on a rope.[1]

In one version the following stanza occurs after the girl's discovery of her pregnancy:

> There is a flower, I've heard folks say,
> That's called a heartsease by night and day,
> I wish I could that flower find
> Would ease my heart, and cure my mind![2]

In others the girl asks for a marble gravestone with a turtle dove carved on it, and several contain the following, or a similar, stanza:

> I wish, I wish—but it's all in vain—
> I wish I was a maid again;
> But a maid again I never must be
> Till an apple grows on an orange-tree.[3]

---

[1] *Journal of the Folk-Song Society*, No. 8, 1906, p. 160.
[2] *Ibid.*, No. 19, 1915, p. 185.
[3] *Ibid.*, p. 182.

THE FOGGY DEW

An interesting variant on stanza 4 ('There is a bird in yonder tree') occurs in a version collected by H. E. D. Hammond and reproduced in the *Journal of the Folk-Song Society*, No. 19, p. 188.

> There was three worms on yonder hill,
> They neither could not hear nor see;
> I wish I'd been but one of them
> When first I gained my liberty.

A note to this text suggests that this is older than the 'bird' version, 'blind bird' being a corruption of 'blind worm'. 'Worm' means any creeping thing, and the deaf worm would be the adder.

THE FOGGY DEW (No. 33)

On account of the variety and confusion of the ms. versions of *The Foggy Dew*, of the intrinsic merits of the song, of the present popularity of a recent version, and of the falsification of its meaning, it may be of interest to consider this song in detail.

In *Folk Songs from Somerset*, I, 1904, Sharp and his collaborator, the Rev. Charles L. Marson, printed the following text:

> One night as I lay in my bed,
>   As I lay fast asleep
> My pretty Love seemed to come to my head
>   And bitterly she did weep.
> She wrung her hands and she tore her hair
>   Crying, asking: What shall I do?
> For they say the love that menfolk bear
> Dries off like the foggy dew, dew, dew,
>   More swift than the foggy dew.
>
> Watch on, dear Love, the lee long night,
>   And the morning will be here;
> Then rise pretty maid and don't be afraid
>   Men love, be it mist or clear.
>   So dry your eyes and kiss me dear
>   As once you used to do:
> For the only cold that you need fear
> Is the chill of the foggy dew, dew, dew,
>   Is the chill of the foggy dew.

THE IDIOM OF THE PEOPLE

> She dried her eyes and the gay sun shone,
>   And the world grew green in the blue.
> For the last of the foggy dew was gone
>   The last of the foggy dew.
> But love was there in the mist and shine
>   The old love, wonder and new.
> O fie, pretty maid, to let eyes like thine
> Be dimmed by the foggy dew, dew, dew,
>   By fear of the foggy dew.

To this they appended the note:

> Mr Marson has re-written the words, retaining as many lines of Mrs Hooper's song as were desirable.

In fact no more than six of the twenty-seven lines are more or less as dictated by the two sisters at Hambridge, in the winter of 1903. This harmless composition, reminiscent of William Morris in his more sentimental vein rather than of any folk song original, completely suppresses the real situation and eliminates the essential spirit of the song. Sharp appears to have thought that in this case Marson went a bit too far, for he did not reprint *The Foggy Dew* in any of his later publications.

The popularity of a different and more authentic version at the present day dates from the appearance of a gramophone record made by Benjamin Britten and Peter Pears shortly after the last war. This is much nearer Sharp's ms. versions, and the authorities evidently endorse Marson's attitude of fifty years ago, since the record is banned from broadcasting in Britain. This is a three-stanza version: the first stanza tells of a young weaver courting a fair young maid in order to save her from the foggy dew. In the second, the girl appears at his bedside in distress—

> So I hauled her into bed and I covered up her head
> Just to keep her from the foggy, foggy dew.

In the third stanza, the girl has disappeared, and the weaver lives with his presumably illegitimate son, who bears a strong resemblance to his mother. The suggestiveness of this version, which may partly account for its present popularity, seems to me out of keeping with the best folk song tradition, in which frankness rather than innuendo is the rule. No symbolic significance is here attached to the title-phrase. 'She sighed, she cried, she damn near died' and 'I hauled her into bed' are probably vulgarisms of comparatively recent date. Mr Britten has been kind enough to tell me that he cannot remember the source of his text but that he believes he got it from a friend who heard it in a Suffolk inn.

Shortly before the war the song was also recorded by the American poet and guitarist Carl Sandburg, whose words consist essentially of only the first and third stanzas of the Britten version. The weaver acquires a son by simply 'wooing' a fair young maid, who makes no direct appearance at all.

> And the only, only thing I did that was wrong
> Was to keep her from the foggy, foggy dew

Mr Sandburg regards this vagueness as a merit. In the notes accompanying the record he says: 'An old somber story is given here without any of the lackadaisical latter-day interpolations. A long novel of lives gone with the wind is epitomized in two verses deep with the night drench of the British Isles.'

It is doubtful whether this view of folk song would have been endorsed by the singers who gave Sharp their songs. To return to Lucy White and Louie Hooper, whose *Foggy Dew* was not considered 'desirable' and which has consequently never been printed—here is their version, unimproved. (See Plate 4, facing p. 53.)

> One night as I lay on my bed
> As I lay fast asleep
> A pretty maid came to my bedside
> Most bitterly she did weep
>
> She wrung her hands and tore her hair
> Crying asking what shall I do?
> Come into my bed my fair pretty maid
> For fear of the foggy dew, dew, dew
> For fear of the foggy dew.
>
> So there they laid all that long night
> Till daylight did appear
> Come rise pretty maid and don't be afraid
> For the foggy dew is gone, gone, gone
> For the foggy dew is gone.

THE IDIOM OF THE PEOPLE

> I never told her all her faults
> And I never do intend so to do
> But there's many a time I've rolled her in my arms
> For fear of the foggy dew, dew, dew
> For fear of the foggy dew
>
> (ms. 87)

This implies a quite different situation; there is an illicit amour but no child; the girl rather than the man is considered to have done wrong; and 'the foggy dew' takes on a more than climatic significance. We are not told why 'fear of the foggy dew' causes the girl such severe emotional disturbance. Clearly these four stanzas leave much unsaid. Unfortunately we do not know whether the singers regarded the song as a complete and satisfying whole, or whether they were repeating something they did not fully understand.

Shortly afterwards Sharp collected from an unnamed source the following version often stanzas:

> Once I was a little boy
> I went to learn my trade
> And all that my delight it was
> in courting of a maid
>
> I courted her one midsummer day
> And part of the winter too
> Until I gained this fair maid's heart
> She knew not what to do
>
> She wrung her hands and tore her hair
> Crying asking what shall I do
> Come into my bed my fair pretty maid
> For fear of the foggy dew, dew, dew
>
> So there they laid all that long night
> Till daylight did appear
> Come rise pretty maid, and don't be afraid
> For the foggy dew is gone
>
> And when she rose and saw the light
> She cries I am undone
> I said fair maid be not afraid
> For the foggy dew is done

THE FOGGY DEW

O when you shall [shall you] come on my dear
O when shall you come on
When oaken leaves fall off the trees
And greener ones come on

Oh that will be too long my dear
Oh that will be too long
My heart will burst, and die I must
That is if you don't come on

The very next day I married her
I married her for life
And ever since I married her
I proved her for my wife

When we have a child my dear
Oh that will make you smile
And when we have another
We will wait a little while

And when we have another my dear
And have another too
Why we must leave off kissing
And think on the foggy dew

(ms. 107)

Here innuendo has 'gone with the wind', and the story is much less shadowy. The seduction of the man by the girl is as in the Britten version, but she also persuades him to marry her, and he is reconciled to the prospect of a considerable family. The reference in the White-Hooper version to the husband's forbearance about his wife's 'faults' is now comprehensible, though it is omitted from the present version. Stanzas 6 and 7, beginning 'O when shall you come on' (that is, 'make me your wife'), are interesting: they occur in no other version, and may well be an accretion from some other source. Yet there is something to be said for retaining them, since they assist the narrative and were evidently considered at some time in the evolution of the song to be relevant. Indeed, it is possible that this version is the oldest we possess; it is certainly more akin than the others to a true ballad.

THE IDIOM OF THE PEOPLE

In 1904 Sharp obtained from a singer named John Voke yet another version:

> When I was young and in my prime
> I carried on the weaving trade
> And all the harm that ever I done
> Was courting a fair pretty maid
> I courted her a long summer's day
> And part of the winter too
> Till I thought it my time to roll her in my arms
> Think no more on the foggy foggy dew.
>
> Last night as I lay on my bed
> I dreamed of a sweet pretty maid
> Last night as I lay on my bed
> She came to my bedside
> She weep, she wailed, she wrung her hands
> Crying O what shall I do?
> Jump into bed my fair pretty maid
> For fear of the foggy foggy dew.
>
> For when you have our child my dear
> It will cause you for to smile
> And when you have another my dear
> It'll cause you to tarry awhile
> And when you have another my dear
> Another and another and two
> You must leave off your roguish tricks
> And think no more on the foggy dew
>
> I never once told her of her faults
> Nor it's never my intention so to do
> And every time she smiled in my face
> Makes me think on the foggy dew

(ms. 297)

Here the singer's memory was obviously at fault, and I do not think he understood the song. There is no hint of marriage, yet clearly a fairly permanent relationship is envisaged. This is the only version in which the girl appears to the young man in a dream. There is once more a reference to the girl's 'faults'. For reasons to

THE FOGGY DEW

be given later, it is obvious that the final line of stanza 3— 'And think no more on the foggy dew'—is corrupt.

Later in the same year Sharp got from Mrs E. Hutchings at Langport another version of which he transcribed only one stanza and one line, concluding with the words 'etc etc (as in other versions)':

> O once I was a bachelor
> I went to learn my trade
> And all that I took delight in was
> A courting a fair pretty maid.
> I courted her one long summer's day
> And a part of the Winter too
> Until I gained this fair pretty maid's heart
> And she knew not what to do do do
> 'Till she knew not what to do.
>
> One night as I lay on my bed
>
> (ms. 350)

The chief interest of this is in the line 'Till she knew not what to do', which confirms the suggestion in other versions that the young man played some part in provoking the girl to seduce him.

In 1908 a further version was obtained from one of Sharp's best sources, William Stokes of Chew Stoke:

> When I was a bachelor young and gay
> I followed the roving trade
> And all the harm that ever I done
> I courted a pretty maid
> I courted her in the summer season
> And part of the winter too
> And many a night I walked with her
> All o'er the foggy dew.
>
> One night as I lay on my bed
> As I lay fast asleep
> Then up came this pretty fair maid
> And most bitterly did weep
> She wept she moaned she tore her hair
> Crying Alas what shall I do,
> This [night] I'm resolved to stay with you
> For fear of the foggy dew.

THE IDIOM OF THE PEOPLE

'Twas in the first part of the night
We passed our time away
And in the later part of the night
For she stayed with me till day
And when broad daylight did appear
She cried I am undone
O hold your Tongue you silly young girl
For the foggy dew has gone.

Suppose that you should have a child
What need have you to fear?
Suppose that you should have another
What need have we to care?
And suppose that we should have another
And another and another one too
'Twould make you think of your foolish tricks
And about the foggy dew.

I loved this girl most dearly
And I loved her as my wife
I took this girl and married her
Made her my lawful wife
And I never told her of her faults
And never intended to do
But every time she smiled at me
I think of the foggy dew.

(ms. 1891)

This gives the story in its fullest form, with the exception of the two 'ballad' stanzas already referred to (ms. 107). It is substantially the same as a broadside in the Nottingham University Library reprinted in *The Common Muse* (Pinto and Rodway, 1957). The following are the principal variations in this broadside:

William Stokes (ms. 1891)	*The Common Muse* (cxciii)
roving trade	weaving trade
pretty maid	servant maid
I walked with her	I rolled her in my arms
We passed our time away	we both did sport and play
For she stayed with me till day	She slept in my arms till day

1577   **Baffled Knight**

As I walked out one May morning
one May morning betime.
There I saw a pretty maid
a floating by the tide
Singing True blue fa ever
True true blue
[illegible] fa ever
How sweet the winds do blow

Take me out of this water
And lay me on the ground
Then you shall have my maidenhead
And twenty thousand pound

He got up on one horse
And she got on the other
So they rode along the road
Like sister & like brother

PLATE 3   A VERSION OF
BLOW AWAY THE MORNING DEW (No. 14)
Facsimile from the Cecil Sharp Mss

The Foggy Dew

One night as I lay on my bed
As I lay fast asleep
A pretty maid came to my bedside
Most bitterly she did weep

She wrung her hands and tore her hair
Crying asking what shall I do?
Come into my bed my fair pretty maid
For fear of the foggy dew, dew, dew
For fear of the foggy dew.

So there they laid all that long night
Till daylight did appear
Come, rise pretty maid and don't be afraid
For the foggy dew is gone, gone, gone
For the foggy dew is gone.

I never told her all her faults
And I never do intend so to do
But there's many a time I've rolled her in my arms
For fear of the foggy dew, dew, dew
For fear of the foggy dew

Lucy White & Louie Hooper at Hambridge
Dec 23. 1903. (51)

PLATE 4 A VERSION OF *THE FOGGY DEW* (No. 33)
Facsimile from the Cecil Sharp Mss

THE FOGGY DEW

William Stokes (ms. 1891)	*The Common Muse* (cxciii)
What need have you to fear?	It would cause us to smile
What need have we to care?	It would make us laugh awhile.
And about the foggy dew	And think no more of the Foggy dew.
But every time she smiled at me	But every time she winks or smiles
I think of the foggy dew	sh(e)th(i)nks of the foggy(dew).[1]

This, I think, is a case in which a printer of broadsides has appropriated a genuine folk song from oral tradition and has made at least one error due to misunderstanding. The line 'And think no more of the Foggy dew' contains the same error as in the Voke version above (ms. 297). It is just possible that the Stokes version (ms. 1891) derives from the broadside, but a common origin seems more likely. I do not think that any of Sharp's versions derives solely from the broadside, and it appears that the song enjoyed considerable popularity in widely divergent forms.[2]

It is because of this divergence that I have quoted and discussed the different versions in full. I have not referred to the innumerable inessential variations, though these argue a vigorous and independent life for the song in different localities.

The main differences centre on the significance attached to the phrase 'foggy dew'. For the question must strike the attentive reader, What is the reason for the almost ritual insistence on this phrase?

It would be well at this point to reconstruct the situation as it emerges from the fuller versions of the song as distinct from the popular derivatives. The story is an unusual one in folk song literature. It is told in the first person, the teller being in some versions a weaver; in others no trade is mentioned, and in one he 'followed the roving trade'. He courts a girl, apparently with no immediate thought of seduction or marriage. The courtship may have begun on a midsummer morning expedition. The girl falls passionately in love with the young man and appears one night at his bedside

---

[1] Line corrupt in ms.
[2] A version recorded for the BBC by Mr Seámus Ennis in 1947 in County Cork has a decidedly literary flavour and is only distantly related to the versions noted by Sharp.

in a state of frenzied agitation. She spends the night in bed with him 'for fear of the foggy dew'; in the morning she is afflicted with remorse, but her lover calms her by telling her that 'the foggy dew is gone'. Shortly afterwards ('the very next day', according to one version) the two are married, and either just before or soon after the marriage they discuss the probable arrival of children. Two babies would be, he tells her, a source of pleasure, but after the birth of two or three more they had better restrain themselves and 'think on the foggy dew'. The man concludes his narrative by admitting that the marriage turned out well despite its inauspicious beginning, and that the recollection of the 'foggy dew' is something of a joke between them. The story varies in detail from version to version, but that is the essential outline. No single version gives the whole story; the composite text I give as No. 33 consists of the essential elements drawn from Sharp's English ms. versions.

What then is the significance of the title-phrase? Its repetition at key moments makes a purely naturalistic explanation unlikely. In any case this would not make sense. If the phrase simply implies the inconvenience of a casual courtship in the open fields, there seems to be no adequate reason for the girl's dramatic appearance at night in a state of hysteria: she would hardly force herself on her lover 'for fear of the damp night air. And why does he console her in the morning for the consequence of her rashness by telling her that 'the foggy dew is gone'? Why, finally, does he tell her that after the birth of a number of children (more perhaps than a poor weaver can maintain) she must abandon her wanton ways and think once more of the foggy dew? If the phrase is taken literally, the song is nonsense.

It is an odd phrase, sufficiently so to make one suspect a verbal corruption. 'Foggy' (and 'fog') occur elsewhere in folk song literature only very occasionally. Yet no attempt to find an Irish or Norman-French equivalent has met with any success. Leaving aside 'foggy', however, we can find plenty of references to 'dew' used symbolically. In all these it is associated with virginity. It is so in the fifteenth-century lyric beginning 'I sing of a maiden that is makeles'. Here dew is mentioned three times, as falling successively on 'grass', 'flower' and 'spray' and thus celebrating the virginity of Mary at each stage in the birth of Jesus.

In Renaissance poetry 'dew' or 'the morning dew' on flowers is the symbol of the virginity they are to lose at the appearance of the male sun. This idea is recurrent in Herrick's Hesperides, where dew is also the tears wept by the flowers for their approaching ravishment. This symbolism would also have been present to the original readers of Marvell's *To his Coy Mistress*:

> Now therefore, while the youthful hue
> Sits on thy skin like morning dew

It is also present in traditional songs such as the several versions of *Blow away the Morning Dew, Dabbling in the Dew* and *Searching for Lambs* (Nos. 14, 24 and 90). The French for 'dew' is 'rosée', and in some regions of France, in a ceremony similar to that of the May Queen in England, a girl awarded a prize for virtue is called a 'rosière'. A very precise use of 'dew' in this sense occurs in an anonymous broadside entitled *The Mower*.[1] This concerns the vain efforts of a young man to take a girl's virginity, and the story is related in strictly symbolic terms, the taking of virginity being represented by mowing a meadow. (This significance is present in other traditional songs about mowing and hay-making.) The second stanza describes the maiden's invitation to the young mower:

> She said, my handsome young man, if a mower that you be,
> I'll find you some new employment if you will go with me,
> For I have a little meadow long kept for you in store,
> It was on the dew, I tell you true, it ne'er was cut before.

'Dew', then, means virginity—or more generally, chastity; and this is the only interpretation which makes sense in every context of *The Foggy Dew*. 'Foggy', however, remains a problem, of which I have discovered no completely satisfactory solution. It *may* be no more than a general epithet characterizing 'dew', but I am inclined to think otherwise.[2] 'Fog' is derived from the Middle English word 'fogge', meaning 'coarse rank grass' of the kind which grows in marshes and bogs where the atmosphere would be damp and misty. The adjective 'foggy' has had at different times several metaphorical senses, including 'murky', 'fuddled', 'tipsy'. The noun 'fogey', whose etymology is doubtful, may be derived from 'fog' or 'foggy',

[1] V. de Sola Pinto and A. E. Rodway: *The Common Muse* (Chatto & Windus, 1957), No. cxlii.
[2] I do not know whether there is any special significance in the capitalization of the word 'Foggy' each time it occurs in the broadside text.

and has also had a variety of meanings, including 'old maid'. I interpret 'foggy dew', then, as 'perpetual chastity'. Moreover, if, in the folk idiom, 'grass' represents 'maidenhead', and the mowing of grass the loss of it, could not 'rank grass' ('fog') stand for 'protracted virginity'?

It is probable that during the later history of this song its original symbolic significance was obscured in the popular mind. In this way the title-phrase was used inconsistently, and confusion resulted. For instance, in the Voke version (ms. 297)

> You must leave off your roguish tricks
> And think no more on the foggy dew

cannot be right; the meaning is rather 'think on the foggy dew' (as in ms. 107, the reading I have adopted). The girl is being told that when she and her husband have had a number of children they must live in chastity once more. This contradiction occurs also in the broadside text.

Finally, as an example of the hopeless confusion resulting from evident misunderstanding of traditional symbolism, it is worth while to quote the single American version which Sharp collected in the Appalachians in 1918 from Ebe Richards in Virginia.

> I courted her all the winter
> And part of the summer too,
> And all the harm that ever I done
> Was to court a pretty fair maid.

> One night she came to my bedside,
> So bitterly she did weep.
> Come to my bed, my pretty fair miss,
> Get out of the foggy dew.

> She laid in my arms till broad daylight,
> The sun began to shine.
> I turned my back on the pretty fair miss.
> Good bye, love, I'm gone.

> Towards the first part of the year
> She took pale in the face.
> Along towards the latter part of the year
> She got bigger around the waist.

THE FOGGY DEW

Along towards the last of the year
She brought me a son.
Now you see as well as I
What the foggy dew has done.

I taken this girl and married her,
I loved her as my life
And I taken this girl and married her,
She made me a virtuous wife.

I never throwed it up to her.
Damn my eyes if I had.
For every time the baby cried
I'd think of the foggy dew.

(ms. 3156)

It might be possible, adopting a literal view of the title-phrase, to argue that this has a rough coherence, but surely it has none of the subtlety or the emotional and psychological interest of the English versions.

ENGLISH TRADITIONAL VERSE

from the manuscripts of

CECIL J. SHARP

NOTE ON THE TEXT

In the following pages I have given the text of each song under the title used by Cecil Sharp in his mss. The arrangement is alphabetical, except in the few instances where variant versions occur under different titles. Immediately after the text appears the page number in the mss., followed by the name of the singer from whom the song was obtained, together with his or her age, if stated, and the place where the song was collected. Then follows a note of the number of other versions of the same song contained in the mss., whether or not these are quoted in the subsequent notes. These sources are enclosed in square brackets.

Next I have given details of textual variants, followed by brief explanatory notes where required. I have added the sources of printed texts, where these exist, and concluded with any general observations which seem to me relevant.

1 *Adieu to Old England*

Adieu to old England Adieu and Adieu
And adieu to some hundreds of pounds
If the world had been ended when I had been young
My sorrows I'd never have known.

Once I could drink of the best
The very best brandy and rum
Now I am glad of a cup of spring water
That flows from Town to Town

Once I could eat of good bread
Good bread that was made of good wheat
Now I am glad with a hard moulded crust
And glad that I got it to eat

Once I could lie on a good bed
A good bed that was made of soft down
Now I am glad of a clot of clean straw
To keep myself from the cold ground

Once I could ride in my carriage
With servants to drive me along
Now I'm in prison in prison so strong
Not knowing which way to turn.

[1177 Jacob Giblett (77) at Westhay 1907. Two other versions]

362   Mrs Lock 1904:

2.1-2   O once I could drink the best beer
       And the beer that was made of fine brown
4.3   But now I am glad of a lock of clean straw

2 An Alderman's Lady

Her master came to her one morning
To play and diddle with her knee
Many fine presents he brought her
Saying Nancy my dearest love me.

Master I wonder much at you
A man of such high degree
For to have such a longing desire
A poor innocent girl to betray

Now 'spose I was to prove by child by you
And you the self same thing deny
Then my dear baby would suffer
And I in some prison should lie

No Nancy you shall go to your mother
She lives in fair Gloucestershire
And your dear little baby I'll murder
There's no one should know it my dear

Then I would not trust you nor try you
Nor neither young man in this place
Not so much as one night to lay by me
You'd bring me to shame and disgrace

When he found he could not delude her
O he took her to church straight away
And Nancy an alderman's lady
She can ride in her carriage so gay.

Now Nancy's an alderman's lady
And she in her carriage can ride
She have servants to wait all upon her
And a footman to ride by her side

AN ALDERMAN'S LADY

[967 John Barnett at Bridgwater 1906]

  5.2 *Nor neither*: 967 Now neither

One other version:

2063 *The Alderman* Jack Barnard at Bridgwater 1909

  2.2 *degree*: 967 degrees.

  3.2 *thing deny*: 967 thing in I.

3 *The Alphabet*

A stands for the apple that grew on the tree
B was the boat that would hold you and me
C was the cat that caught all the mice and
D was the doll dressed up very nice
E was the Eagle and chained to the perch
F stands for Fanny returning from church
G was the gardiner a-working many hours and
H was the hothouse that held his choice flowers
I was the Indian with his arrow and bow
J was the Jackdaw I very well know
K was the Keeper who fed the wild beasts
L was the Lion and none of the least
M was the Magpie who could say all it heard
N noisy Nancy who would have the last word
O was the ostler whose horse was his pride and
P was the pony that William could ride
Q was the Queen dressed up all so grand
R was the Rabbit that fed from her hand.
S was the ship that was laded with gold
T was the Turk who was warlike and bold
U was my Uncle with his new umberello
V was the Valet quite a compleasant fellow
W was the Welshman just returned from Wales
X was the shape of a windmill's four sails
Y was the youth who could bear with a grace
Z the new Zealander with his fine figured face.

[2207 Mrs Beecher at Shipston Workhouse 1910. No other version]

4 *American Stranger*

A

I have been a rambling by night and by day
But to prove myself riyals I will gang along with you
And I will take you to Amerikee
O my darling to be.

Some says I'm ragged
Some says I am poor
But to prove myself riyals I will gang along with you

O in the middle of the ocean
Then shall grow a maypole tree
If ever I prove false
To the girl that loves me

Kind love to my Polly
Although she is poor
Give my love to my Betsy
She's the girl I adore
I'll roll her in my arms
On a cold winter's night

And I wandered from my darling
For many a long mile
Now our ship it is ready
'Tis ready to set sail
And I'll take you to Amerikee
My darling to be
And when we gets over to our own Countree
We'll drink the good health to the Indian Lass.

AMERICAN STRANGER

B

I am a stranger in this country from America I came
There is no one that knows me nor can tell my name
I have wandered from my darling a many long mile

Some says I'm rakish some says I'm wild
Some says I'm foolish my mind to beguile
But to prove myself royal you should come along with me
And I'll take you to America my darling to be

The moon shall be in darkness and the sun give no light
If ever I prove false to my own heart's delight
In the middle of the ocean there shall grow a myrtle tree
If ever I prove false to the girl that loves me.

[A 1335 Mrs Priscilla Carper at Stafford Common 1907

    1.2 *riyals*: cf. royal in B 2.3: loyal.

B 1872 Thomas Downing at Marylebone Workhouse 1908]
(One other distantly related version was noted in America)

    3.1 *the moon shall be in darkness*: cf. Ecclesiastes xii. 2.
3.3 *myrtle*: symbol of constant love (as in Searching for Lambs, No. 90).
    3.4 *girl*: 1872 girls.

Sharp printed B in the *Journal of the Folk-Song Society*, No. 18, omitting the third verse. Vaughan Williams printed the first verse of a similar version in the *Journal of the Folk-Song Society*, No. 13, adding 'The rest of the words need not be printed'.

5 *Arthur Bradley O*

'Twas in the month of May
The maidens they did say
That a maypole they would have
And one that is fine and brave
Silly Bob put off his hat
For he be called a sap
(That every man should show)
For his name was Arthur a Bradley O
Hooroo boys Hooroo for his name was Arthur
    Bradley O.

As Arthur walked forth one day
He met Dorothy by the way
He took her by the hand
Desired that she should stand
Saying if s'ever thee loved thee mother
Love I and love no other
For love it will conquer a king
And a sorrowful heart it will bring
For her name was Draggletail Dorothy O.
Hooroo etc.

Well a courting Arthur went
It was against his friends' consent
His sweetheart had but one eye
Her nose stood all awry
Mouth from ear to ear
With a hump upon her back
And kissing she did not lack
And bandy legs she was
That a wheelbarrow may go through
And it's hooroo boys
For her name it was Draggletail Dorothy O
Hooroo etc.

ARTHUR BRADLEY O

Well a wedding we must have
And one that is fine and brave
We'll ask the neighbours round
One out of every town
There's old Mother Wick to Bob
Old Grandmother Squid to squob
In steps old Hannah Sutten
She got a roasting of mutten
In steps old Hannah Don
With
    [three lines of dashes]

When death is pleased to call
I'll swear I'll leave thee all
There's barrels and buckets and loons
And a half dozen old iron spoons
And two old left handed mittens
Besides an old curtain ring
And a half dozen old brass buttons
Tied up on a leather string
And a chimney pot so good
That ever was made with wood
And something else is left to my lot
That's a good old mustard pot
Her name it was Draggletail Dorothy O
Hooroo boys etc.

[3374 Mr Richard Bond at Idbury, Oxon. 1923. One other version]
  1.6 *a sap*: possibly, to sup.
  2.9. *Draggletail*: possibly a gypsy (cf. Raggle-taggle).

This seems to be a comparatively late version of a comic song which had been printed as early as the seventeenth century. The hero is mentioned in one of the *Robin Hood* ballads and in plays by Jonson and Dekker.

6 *As I walked through the Meadows*

Young Johnny was a plough boy, so fresh as a rose
And so sweet-lie sang unto his plough
While blackbirds and thrushes on every green bough
While the dairymaid sat milking her cow

He took this fair maid by her lily white hand
Through the meadows they wandered away
He placed his true love on a green mossy bank
While he gathered her a handful o' sweet may

And when he returned to her she gave to him a smile
And she thanked him for what he had done
He spreaded the sweet may on her lilywhite breast
But believe me Sir there never growed no thorn

'Twas early next morning he made her his bride
That the world may have nothing to say
The bells they shall ring and the birds sweetly sing
While he crowned her the Queen of sweet may.

[15 Louie Hooper and Lucy White at Hambridge 1903]

One of nine versions, all more or less parallel, some having the following additional verse at the beginning:
    Cold winter's gone and past; pleasant summer's come at last
    And the meadows are pleasant and gay
    The lark in the morning so sweetly she sung
    And the small birds on every green spray
      (745 John Vincent at Priddy 1905)

  2.4 *he*: omitted in 15.
  3.2 *he had done*: she had done, in 15.
  3.4 *there never growed no thorn*: i.e. the courtship was chaste.

Sharp printed this song verbatim in the *Journal of the Folk-Song Society*, No. 6, 1905, and quite different versions in *Folk Songs from Somerset*, I, 1904, and II, 1905.

7 *As I was going to Banbury*

As I was going to Banbury
   Ri fol latitee O
As I was going to Banbury
I saw a fine coddlin apple tree
   With a ri fol latitee O.

And when the coddlins began to fall
I found five hundred men in all

And one of the men I saw was dead
So I sent for a hatchet to open his head

And in his head I found a spring
And seven young salmon a learning to sing

And one of the salmon as big as I
Now do you not think I am telling a lie?

And one of the salmon as big as an elf
If you want any more you must sing it yourself.

[1957 Sister Emma (71) at Clewer 1909]

A children's riddle song printed by Sharp in Novello's *School Songs,* 1909. According to the editors of *The Oxford Dictionary of Nursery Rhymes,* 'The fact that so many nursery pieces mention Banbury may, in part, be due to the energy of the printer, Rusher. Working at Banbury he often altered the wording to suit local patronage, but his influence was more than local.'

8 *Banks of Claudy*

As I walked out one morning
All in the month of May
Down through some flower gardens
So I carelessly did stray
I overheard a damsel
In sorrow to complain
All for her absent lover
That ploughs the raging main.

I stepped up to this fair maid
I put her in surprise
I own she did not know me
I being dressed in disguise
Says I my lovely maiden
My joy and heart's delight
How far have you to wander
This dark and dreary night?

All the way Kind Sir to Claddy
If you will please to show
Pity a poor girl distracted
It's there I have to go.
I'm in search of a faithless young man
And Johnny is his name
And on the banks of Claddy
I'm told he does remain.

If my Johnny he was here this night
He'd keep me from all harm
But he's in the field of battle
All in his uniform
He's in the field of battle
His foes he will destroy
Like a roving King of honour
He fought on the banks of Troy.

BANKS OF CLAUDY

O 'tis six months and better
Since your Johnny left the shore
He's a cruising the wide ocean
Where foaming billows roar.
He's a cruising the wide ocean
For honour and for gain
The Ship's been wrecked as I am told
All on the coast of Spain.

As soon as she heard him say so
She fell into deep despair
By wringing of her milk white hands
And tearing of her hair
If my Johnny he be drownded
No man on earth I'll take
But through lonesome groves and valleys
I will wander for his sake.

As soon as he heard her say so
He could no longer stand
But he fell into her arms
Saying Bessie I'm the man
I am that faithless young man
Whom you thought was slain
And once we've met on Claddy banks
We'll never part again.

[378 Mrs Slade 1904. No other version]

 1.7 *All*: 378 Nor
 4.7 Like a roving King of honour
   He fought on the banks of Troy.

A version in the *Journal of the Folk-Song Society*, No. 13, 1909, has:
   Like the royal king of honour upon the walls of Troy.
Sharp did not publish this song. Parallel versions were noted by Kidson and others.

9 *The Banks of Green Willow*

It's of a sea captain down by the sea side.
He courted a young damsel and got her by child

Go and get your mother's will O and all your father's money
To sail across the ocean along with your Johnny

I've got my father's will O and all my mother's money
To sail across the ocean along with my Johnny

We had not sailed miles no not great many
Before she was delivered of a beautiful baby

Go and get me a white napkin to tie my head easy
To throw me quite overboard both me and my baby

Now see how she totters now see how she tumbles
Now see how she's rolling all on the salt water

Go and get me a long boat to row my love back again
To row my love back again both she and her baby

Now she shall have a coffin a coffin shall shine yellow
And she shall be buried on the Banks of Green Willow

The bells shall ring mournful O for my dearest Polly
And she shall be buried for the sake of her money

[502 Elizabeth Mogg 1904. Five other versions]

One of six versions noted by Sharp, all evidently incomplete but roughly parallel. In some the captain takes the initiative in throwing the woman overboard, and there is no mention of a rescue but only of a coffin edged with yellow (i.e. gold). In others money is not introduced until she offers him a sum to turn the ship and bring her back to shore; he refuses on the ground that to do so would be to risk the lives of all on board. A much fuller version is given by Child, in which the reason for casting out the woman is that her presence is believed to have put a curse on the ship. In publishing the song in *Folk Songs from Somerset*, I, 1904, Sharp supplemented his ms. version from printed ballad sources.

10 *The Basket of Eggs*

Three jolly sailors set out a walking
With their pockets lined with gold
As they were walking, so kindly a-talking
Two lovely maidens they did behold.

I said pretty maidens shall I carry your basket
The answer it was, kind sir if you please
Sailors O sailors if you should outwalk me
Leave it at the inn called the 'Chaise and pair'

Oh landlord, O landlord fetch me some bacon
Eggs in the basket and we'll have a fry
The Landlord he went searching the basket
Thinking eggs there for to find

Oh sailors, oh sailors you are mistaken
Instead of eggs it is a young babe

One of them set out a prattling
The other he said wait awhile
Here's fifty pound I will pay down
If anyone will own this child

Then up spoke one called Lovely Nancy
That I danced with last Easter day
I'll take the child and so kindly use it
If the money you will pay.

[894 Mrs Laurence at Somerton 1906. No other version]

The *Journal of the Folk-Song Society,* No. 2, 1900, prints a text essentially the same but rather fuller. It is connected with another song, not noted by Sharp, called *The Oyster Girl.*

11 Bessy Bingle

Bessy Bingle had a little pig
It was so little because it was not big
It was so little it lived in a scuttle
And one day she found it as dead as a shuttle

Bessy Bingle she laid down and cried
Johnny Bingle he laid down and died
And here is an end of one two and three
Johnny Bingle, Bessy Bingle and the little piggee.

[1954 Sister Emma at Clewer 1909. No other version]

A parallel version entitled *Little Betty Pringle* is given in *The Oxford Dictionary of Nursery Rhymes*, 1951.

12 *Billy Boy*

Is she fitting for your wife Billy Boy
　Billy Boy
Is she fitted for your wife Billy Boy?
She's fitted to my wife
As the haft is to the knife
She's my Nancy, please-my-fancy
I'm her charming Billy Boy

Did she ask you to sit down Billy Boy
　Billy Boy
Did she ask you to sit down Billy Boy?
Yes she asked me to sit down
And she curtsied to the ground
She's my Nancy, please-my-fancy
I'm her charming Billy Boy

Did she light you up to bed Billy Boy
　Billy Boy
Did she light you up to bed Billy Boy?
Yes she light me up to bed
With the bowing of her head
She's my Nancy, please-my-fancy
I'm her charming Billy Boy

Did she lay so close to you Billy Boy
　Billy Boy
Did she lay so close to you Billy Boy?
Yes she lay so close to me
As the rind unto the tree
She's my Nancy, please-my-fancy
I'm her charming Billy Boy

[271 Mrs Lizzie Welch at Hambridge 1904. Two other versions]

Billy Boy and its near relation *My Boy Billy* have for two centuries been known as a comic song, a children's song and a sea shanty, but the above version has never, so far as I know, been printed. Sharp published a version suitable for children in Novello's *School Songs*, 1912, and in *English Folk Songs*, Selected Edition, 1921, Vol. I. Sharp regarded it as a burlesque of *Lord Rendal*

75

13 Bird Starver's Cry

Hi! Shoo all o' the birds
    Shoo aller birds
    Shoo aller birds

Out of master's ground
Into Tom Tucker's ground

Out of Tom Tucker's ground
Into Tom Tinker's ground

Out of Tom Tinker's ground
Into Luke Collis' ground

Out of Luke Collis' ground
Into Bill Vater's ground

Hi! Shoo aller birds
Kraw! Hoop!

[282 John Durbin at Harptree 1904]

  One other version:
281 John Parnell, East Harptree 1904

  1 Shoo aller birds you be so black
    When I lay down to have a nap

Sharp printed both versions in the *Journal of the Folk-Song Society*, No. 6, 1905, adding the following note: 'Mrs Kettlewell of Harptree Court tells me that "Hi shoo all 'er birds" is the regular cry of the boys who go bird starving in the neighbourhood of Harptree.'

14 *Blow away the Morning Dew*

A

'Twas of a brisk young farmer
Kept sheep all on a hill
And he went out of a May morning
To see what he could kill
    And it's aye the dewy morning
    Blow the wind I ho
    Blow the wind of a dew morning
    How sweet the winds do blow

He gazed high he gazed low
He gave an underlook
And there he saw a fair pretty maid
A bathing in the brook.

It's better for young ladies
To be sewing their silken seams
Than it is to be out of a May morning
A swimming against the stream

It's better for young farmers
To be minding their business at home
Than it is to be out of a May morning
To see young ladies swim

O do not touch my mantle
Pray leave my clothes alone
But take me out of the water
And carry me to my home

She mounted on a milk white steed
And he all on another
They rode along together
Like sister and like brother

BLOW AWAY THE MORNING DEW

They rode along together
Till they came to some cocks of hay
Saying isn't this a pretty place
For girls and boys to play?

O take me to my father's house
And you may sit me down
And you shall have my maidenhead
And fifteen hundred pound

And when she came to her father's gate
So lively she did run
None was so ready as the waiting maid
To let this lady in

Now when she came to her father's gate
She turned herself about
Saying I am a maid within
And thou art a fool without

There is a cock in father's barton
He never tread a hen
He flies about and flutters his wings
And I think you're one of them

There is a herb in father's garden
And some do call it rue
It causes all the girls in autumn
To have a laugh at you

My mother got a flower in her garden
Called Marigold
If you will not when you may
You shall not when you will

A
[494 Mrs Price at Compton Martin 1904
2043 Captain Lewis at Minehead 1909
1783 Mr James Beale (72) at Wareham, Kent 1908]

A composite text using all the elements from the above three parallel versions, none of which is substantially better than the others.

BLOW AWAY THE MORNING DEW
B

As I walked out one May morning
To view the fields all round sir
And there I spied a pretty little maid
All on the new mown hay sir
    Fol the dol a day

I asked of her if I should lay her down
All on the new mown hay sir
And answer that she gave to me
I'm afraid it will not do sir

There is a dew all on the ground
That will spoil my cambric gown O
Which cost my father out of his purse
So many a pound and crown O

There is a wind come from the north
That will blow away all dew O
And I will spread my riding coat
All on the new mown hay O

And if you go to my father's yard
When it's walled all around sir
And there you shall have the will of me
And thirty thousand pound sir

If you come to my father's house
When the moon shines bright and clearly
I will arise and let you in
And no one shall not hear me

I went unto her father's house
When the moon shone bright and clearly
O then she looked and smiled on me
And showed me out of doors sir

There is a cock in my father's yard
He will not tread the hen sir
And I really believe in all my heart
That thou art the same sir

BLOW AWAY THE MORNING DEW

There is a shrub in my father's yard
It's called the merry girl sir
If young men want[1] to when they can
They shall not when they will sir

When you met me in that field
You thought you met a fool sir
Go take your bible in your hand
Go a little more to school sir

You may pull off your shoes and hose
And let your feet go bare O
And if you meet with a pretty girl
You touch her if you dare O

If you should meet with a pretty girl
As you are going home sir
You must never mind the squeaks and the squalls
Or the rumpling of her gown O

B
[1417 Mr Smithers (61) at Tewkesbury 1908
716 John Dingle at Coryton 1905
1574 Charles West (83) at Raskill, Bromfield 1908]

A composite text using the above three versions.

C

As I walked out one May morning
One May morning betime
There I saw a pretty maid
A floating by the tide
    Singing True blue for ever
    True true blue
    King George for ever
    How sweet the winds do blow

[1] i.e. fail

BLOW AWAY THE MORNING DEW

Take me out of this water
And lay me on the ground
Then you shall have my maidenhead
And twenty thousand pound

He got up on one horse
And she got on the other
So they rode along the road
Like sister and like brother

As they rode along the road
They saw a field of grass
Isn't this a pretty place
If you brought your bottle and glass

As they rode along the road
They saw a field of hay
Isn't this a pretty place
For you and me to play?

There's a flower in my father's garden
It's called the marigold
You would not when you could my boy
You shall not now you will

There's a cock in my father's barton
That run among the hens
He often crow and never tread
I think you're much the same

When she came to her father's gate
She nimbly stepped in
You're a fool without these gates
And I'm a maid within

C
[1577 Jack Barnard at Bridgwater 1908]
A full account of this song is given in the Introduction, pp. 40–43.

15 *Blow the Wind Whistling*

Up jumps the salmon
The largest o' em all
He jumps on our fore deck
Saying: Here's meat for all.
    O blow the wind whistling
    O blow the winds all
    Our ship is still hearted boys
    How steady she go!

Up jumps the shark
The largest of all
He jumped on our fore deck:
You should die all.

Then up jumps the sprat
The smallest of all
He jumps on our foredeck
Saying we shall be drowned all.

[210 Louie Hooper at Hambridge 1904. One other version]
    1.3 *on*: 210 in.
    1.7 *still*:? a corruption of steel.

Sharp printed this in the *Journal of the Folk-Song Society*, No. 18, 1914

16 *The Boatsman and the Tailor*

It was an old boatsman down in Dover he did dwell
And he had a little wife and he loved her so well
But when the old boatsman he got out of the way
His frolicsome young wife with some tailor she would lay
   To my rally dally da do rally dally day (*bis*)

Now she was a walking down through the street
This pretty little tailor she chanced for to meet
Saying my husband's gone on board with the rest of his crew
And now this very night I will lie along with you

Then straight away home this couple they did go
A kissing and courting and loving also
But they hadn't been to bed about an hour by the clock
Before the old boatsman at the door he did knock

Now you get into my husband's chest and there you lie still
And then you'll be so safe as any mouse in the mill
And then she went downstairs for to let her husband in
And there stood the boatsman with three of his men

Now what has brought you here so late in the night
You've put the little tailor in a terrible fright
Why I have not a come to rob you nor disturb you of your
   rest
But since I have come here I must have my chest

Now these three able fellows being so stout and strong
They took up the chest and carried it along
But they hadn't carried the chest but a mile outside the town
Before the heft of the chest made the sweatings to run down

Says one to the other let us sit down and rest
Says one to the other why the devil's in the chest
Says one to the other I heard something knock
Then up jumps the old boatsman and his chest he did unlock

THE BOATSMAN AND THE TAILOR

Now the chest he did unlock and was greatly surprised
To see the little tailor all rubbing of his eyes
Saying hullo my little fellow and how came you here
Well you cuckoled me ever this last seven year

Now I'll press you to the seas and a slave thou shalt be
And if I don't sweat thee there the devil shall sweat me
Now I'll press you to the seas and a slave thou shalt be
Thou shalt never stay at home to make a cuckold of me

16   Charles Neville at East Coker 1908. No other English version; two American versions differing from 1666 only in detail]

235 Mrs Sands at Allan Stand, North Carolina 1916:

    43-4 She trippled downstairs and she opened the door
           And in come her husband and three or four more
    5.2 *You've put the little tailor*: it must be supposed that she said this to herself.
    6.4 *heft*: weight.

This merry tale from East Coker is in a vigorous tradition, and, so far as I can discover, has never been printed before. In *English Folk Songs*, Selected Edition, 1921, Vol. II, Sharp describes the words of *The Boatsman and the Tailor* as 'boisterous and unprintable', and appropriates what he calls its 'fine air' to another set of words, *The Green Wedding*.

17 *The Bold Grenadier*

A

As I was a walking one morning in May
I saw a fair couple as they was walking this way
The one was a fair maid and a beauty I declare
And the other was a soldier of a bold grenadier

Kind kisses and compliments as they both did walk together
Till they both did come down by the side of some river
When they did sit down together by the clear crystal stream
Hark hark said the fair maid how the nightingales sing

Where he softly clasped his arms all round her middle
And out of his knapsack he pulled out a fiddle
He played her such a tune my boys that made the valley ring
Hark hark said the fair maid how the nightingales sing

And now said the soldier its time to give over
O no said the fair maid we will have one tune more
For I do like your tune so well and the touch of your string
Hark hark said the fair maid how the nightingales sing

And now for the inn I'm bound for to steer
Where we can drink wine my boys instead of strong beer
And if ever I do return again it shall be early in the spring
To see the pretty flowers grow and hear the nightingales sing.

B

One morning, one morning, one morning in May,
I met a fair couple a-making their way;
One was a lady so neat and so fair
The other a soldier, a brave volunteer.

Good morning, good morning, good morning to thee.
Now where are you going, my pretty lady?
I'm a-going a-walking to the banks of the sea,
To see the waters a-gliding and hear the nightingales sing.

THE BOLD GRENADIER

They hadn't been standing but one hour or two
Till out of his knapsack his fiddle he drew,
And the tune that he played made the valleys to ring.
See the waters a-gliding and hear the nightingales sing.

Pretty lady, pretty lady, 'tis time to give o'er.
O no, pretty soldier, please play one tune more.
I'd rather hear your fiddle by the touch of one string
Than see the waters a-gliding and hear the nightingales sing.

Then, pretty soldier, will you marry me?
O no, pretty lady, that can never be.
I have a wife in London and children twice three.
Two wives in the army is too many for me.

I'll go back to London and stay there one year
And drink all my living in whisky and beer;
And if ever I return it will be in the spring,
See the waters a-gliding and hear the nightingales sing.

[A 1 128 Jim Proll at Monksilver 1906
B 2654 Chester Lewis of Harlan Co., Kentucky 1917
   Three other English versions, one other American]

Another English version has the following two stanzas in place of the final stanza in A.
1437 Alfred Emery at Othery 1908:
   O soldier said the fair maid will you marry me
   O no said the soldier that can never be
   For I've got a wife t'home in my own countrie
   And she's as nice a woman as ever you see

   Now I'm bound to the Indies and there to remain
   For the space of three long years crossing the ocean again
   But if ever I do return again it shall be in the spring
   For to see the pretty flowers grow hear the nightingales sing

For 1437 1.4. another English version (704) has
   So fine and clever a woman as ever you can see
Version B, published in *Folk Songs of the Appalachian Mountains*, Second Series, under the title *The Nightingale*, is American, and is here given for the sake of comparison. The more conventional punctuation is due to the fact that the American songs are not in Sharp's hand but typed by Miss Karpeles. The second American version ends with a characteristic piece of prudential moralizing:

THE BOLD GRENADIER

2944 Mrs Leona Melton at Hyden, Kentucky 1917:
  Come all you young ladies, take warning by me,
  Don't ever set your affections on a soldier so tree;
  For they will deceive you as one deceived me.
  Put you down to the cradle, rock a bye, baby.

18 *Bold Robinson*

Come all you young fellows
That delight in a little game
Come listen unto me
And I will tell you plain
It's of two champions bold
They fought for a sum of gold
And their talk was that young Robinson
Was sure to win the day
    Young Tiley Huzzoo
    Brave Tiley Huzzoo
    Brave Robinson for ever
    And young Tiley Huzzoo

Their stage it had been builded
And the champions on the ground
And fifty bright guineas
These champions did put down
And for fifty bright guineas
These champions they did play
And all the talk was Robinson
Would sure to win the day
    With young Tiley *etc.*

BOLD ROBINSON

'Twas in the fourteenth round
These two champions they did meet
With their bodies sorely wounded
And their hearts full of grief
When all of a sudden Tiley gave
Brave Robinson a blow
Saying I will be the champion
Wherever I do go
   Brave Tiley *etc.*

The battle it being over
And young Tiley he had won
A rich lady fell in love with him
For what he had done.
And if he do recover
A gay wedding shall be seen
But young Tiley he died
At the end of the game
   And did young Tiley Huzzoo
   Brave Robinson Huzzoo
   And the ladies went in mourning
   For young Tiley Huzzoo.

[1090 William Stokes at Chew Stoke 1906. Two other incomplete versions]

19 *The Brisk Young Bachelor*

Once I was a brisk young bachelor
Till my mind was never content
For the want of a wife for to lie by me
To keep me quiet and a sober life
   With my whack fal lor, the diddle and the dido,
   Whack fal lor, the diddle-i-day.

The very first year as we was married
Scarce one hour could I get to sleep
She rubbed my shins till the blood did twinkle
Crying out husband are you asleep?

THE BRISK YOUNG BACHELOR

Home comes I both wet and weary
No dry clothes for to put on
Right upstairs and down in the corner
With the kettle I must run

And if I scarcely make an answer
She will say 'tis come come come
The women say they will have pleasure
Poor man's labour is never a done

Well the second year as we was married
A very fine baby we had born
She forsook it and I took to it
Wropped it up to keep it warm

Away to the alehouse she runs bawling
Like some donkey rattling home
And into my face her hands come slip slap
A poor man's sorrow just begun

[1307 Robert Parish at Exford 1907
2130 Shepherd Hayden (83) at Bampton in the Bush 1909. No other version]

 2.1 *The very first year as we was married*: 1307 The first half year that I was married
 3.4 *kettle*: cant term for female sexual organ (Partridge).

The refrain is given in the ms. as simply 'With my whack fol etc.' I have adopted the full text from Sharp's *English Folk Songs: Selected Edition*, 1921, Vol. II. Apart from these two emendations the text given above combines the whole of 1307 and stanzas 4 and 5 of 2130, which in other respects is substantially parallel.

Sharp collected a number of songs about matrimonial problems, for example *Single Men's Warning* (No. 95). The specific problem here dealt with is treated from the wife's point of view in *O Dear O* (No. 67); another song about an inadequate husband is *The Dandy Man* (No. 25). Another group of songs deals with the question of cuckoldry. Only one song (*Good Old Man*, No. 36) celebrates marital compatibility.
 The text of *The Brisk Young Bachelor* printed by Sharp in the work mentioned above avoids all mention of sexual difficulties.

20 *A Brisk Young Lover*

A brisk young lover came a courting me
He stole away my liberty
He stole it away with a free good will
Although he's false I love him still

All down in the meadows and she did run
A gathering flowers all as they sprung
Of every sort she plucked she pulled
Until she had her apron full

When I wore my apron low
My love followed me through frost and snow
When I wore it up to my chin
My love passed by and never looked in

There is a bird in yonder tree
Some says he's blind and he cannot see
I wish it had been the same by me
Before I had gained my love's company

I wish to God my babe was born
Set smiling on its daddy's arms
And I myself all in the cold clay
And the green grass growing over me.

There is an ale house in yonder town
Where my love goes and sits himself down
He takes some strange girl on his knee
And he tells her what he don't tell me

A grief to me and I'll tell you why
Because she's got more gold than I
Her gold will waste and her beauty will pass
And she will come like me at last

A BRISK YOUNG LOVER

I went upstairs to make the bed
I laid me down and nothing said.
My mistress came and to me said:
What is the matter with you, my maid?

O mistress O mistress if you did know
The pain and sorrows I undergo
Clap your right hand on my left breast
My panting heart can take no rest

There is a man on yonder hill
He's got two hearts like iron and steel
He's got two hearts in the room of one
What a rogue he'll be till he's dead and gone

O take this letter to him with speed
And give it to him that he can read
And bring me an answer without delay
For he has stolen my poor heart away

She took this letter immediately
He read it over while she stood by.
And soon he did this letter burn,
Leaving this maid to grieve and mourn.

What a silly young girl O then she must be
To think that I love no one but she
Man was not made for one alone
I take a delight to hear her moan

Then she returned immediately
And found her maid as cold as clay.
O wicked man, how cruel thou art
For breaking of my own tell's heart.

I'll gather grass for her bed
And a flowery pillow for her head
And the leaves that blow from tree to tree
They shall be the coverlets over she.

A BRISK YOUNG LOVER

O when the sad news to her lover did go
Which made his very blood run cold
I'm glad said he that she died so well
For I longs to hear that mournful bell

O cruel young man as I know thou art
For breaking of that fair one's heart
In Abraham's bosom she shall sleep
Whilst thy tormenting poor soul shall weep

[455 Mrs Overd 1904
1745 Charles Ash at Crowcombe 1908
2209 Robert Feast at Ely Union 1911. ('His grandmother used to sing when ninety years old—101 when she died': Sharp's note.)
3333 Mr William Carpenter at Ross Workhouse 1921
219 William Speening at He Bruers 1904
1058 William Bailey at Carrington 1906
1496 Mrs Elizabeth Smithered (65) at Tewkesbury 1908
1733 Amos Ash at Combe Florey 1908]
(Three other English versions and four American)

The above versions are given under the various titles of *A Brisk Young Lover*, *A Brisk Young Sailor*, *A Brisk Young Man he Courted Me*, *Sheffield Park*, and *In Castle Park*.

This is a composite text using all the above numbered versions. (For a fuller account see Introduction, pp. 43–45.)

3.1 For the connection of 'apron' with pregnancy, see also Nos. 29, 75 and 103.
   10.4 *till*: 2209 when
   14.4 *tell*: as in ms. (3333). Possibly a copyist's error for a girl's name, e.g. Doll, Nell.
   17.3 *Abraham's bosom*: see the parable of Dives and Lazarus (Luke xvi, 22).

21 The Broomfield Wager

A squire a squire he lived in the wood
He courted a lady gay
A little while and he passed a joke
And a wager he did lay.

A wager a wager I'll lay to any man
A thousand guineas to one
That a maid won't go to the merry green woods
And a maid return again.

O when she came to the merry green woods
She found her love asleep
With a knife in his hand and a sword by his side
And a greyhound at his feet.

Three times she walked all round his head
Three times all round his feet
Three times she kissed his red rosy cheeks
As he lay fast asleep.

She took the ring from her finger
Put it on his right hand
That he might know when he did awake
That his love had been there and gone.

And when she done all what she could
She walked softly away
She hied herself in the merry green wood
To hear what her love did say.

When he waked out from his dream
He looked up in the skies
He looked round and round and down on the ground
And he wept most bitterly.

THE BROOMFIELD WAGER

Up he called his serving man
Whom he loved so dear
Why hasn't thou awakened me
When my true love was here.

And with my voice I hallooed master
And with my bells I rung
Awake awake and awake master
Your true love's been and gone.

If I'd been awake when my true love were here
I know I'd a had my will
Or else these birds in yon green 'ood
On her should have had their fill

Sleep more in the night master
And wake more in the day
And then you will see when your true love come
And when she goes away

[1189 William Briffet at Bridgwater 1907
344 Mrs Overd at Langport 1904
    Four other versions, three mere fragments]

  5 This stanza interpolated from 344
  6.3 *hied*:? or 'hide'
  10 as in 344.1189 has the following confused reading:
    I wish I had my true love here
    As free as I've got my will
    And every bird in the merry green wood
    For they should have their fill

Bell reprinted (1857) a full and detailed broadside text of *The Merry Broomfield; or, The West Country Wager*, which he said was the original ballad. The verse is a kind of literary doggerel. He describes as a 'modern antique' Sir Walter Scott's text reprinted by Child as *The Broomfield Hill*. Child says that the ballad is widely dispersed. In Scott's version there is no wager; the lady has an assignation with the knight, which she is afraid to keep for fear of losing her maidenhead. She is instructed by a witch how to keep her lover asleep by means of the magical properties of broom flowers, whose perfume was supposed to be a narcotic. She thus visits him in the wood without his knowledge. When he wakes, he upbraids his horse and his hawk for not having told him of her presence. The horse replies that he had stamped and jingled his harness, the

THE BROOMFIELD WAGER

hawk that he had clapped his wings and rung his bells. (It is evidently the hawk's bells which have been ascribed to the serving man in stanza 9, above.) The knight threatens to throw the horse's carcase to the birds if he does not overtake the lady; but pursuit is useless.

Child also gives a version from Herd (1769) in which the wager is introduced.

The story according to Bell is based on a wager; neither witch nor horse is introduced, but hawk, hound and serving man are all reproved for failing to wake the lover (no longer a 'knight', but a 'noble young squire'). The element of witchcraft is almost entirely suppressed. Bell's statement that his broadside version antedates Scott's cannot be substantiated.

Sharp printed the above version in the *Journal of the Folk-Song Society*, No. 15, 1910, p. 112, but did not publish it. It seems to me to stem from an 'original', older and more authentic than Bell's text. In the other versions noted by Sharp and other collectors the lady's behaviour while her lover is asleep varies considerably: in one she kisses him nine times, but does not walk round him; in another she not only does this but also walks round his head and his feet nine times, and takes the ring from his little finger; in some, but not in all, she gathers broom and strews it on him. In one version, possibly derived from an Italian source, the magic is, in Child's phrase, 'vulgarized into a sleeping draught'.

In an East Anglian text given by Thomas Wood, *Journal of the Folk-Song Society*, No. 33, 1929, p. 127, the lover reacts more savagely on waking:

> Had I been awake instead of being asleep,
> And could not have gained my will,
> All these wild birds on this bonny broom field,
> This night should have had their fill.
>
> Her blood should have been their drink for them,
> Her flesh should have been their meat;
> Her bones would have been their pillow by night,
> When they lay them down to sleep.

22 Cold Blow and a Rainy Night

My hat is frozen to my head
My body's like a lump of lead
My shoes are frozen to my feet
Standing at your window
    Let me in the soldier cried
    Cold blow and a rainy night
    Let me in the soldier cried
    I'll never go back again, O.

Down she came and let him in
And then they went to bed again
He kissed her lips and tickled her knee
And soon he gained her favour
    Then she blessed the rainy night
    Cold blow and a rainy night
    Then she blessed the rainy night
    That ever she let him in O

O lad, O lad, O marry me
My father will give thee gold so free
O no, O no I'll not marry
So fare you well for ever
    Then she cursed the rainy night
    Cold blow and a rainy night
    Then she cursed the rainy night
    That ever she let him in O

Then he jumped out of bed
He put his hat upon his head
And she had lost her maidenhead
Her mother heard the jingle.
    Then she cursed the rainy night
    Cold blow and a rainy night
    Then she cursed the rainy night
    That ever she let him in O.

[1785 James Beale at Wareham, Kent 1908. No other version]
    4.4 *jingle*: cf. refrain of No. 34, *Gently Johnny my Jingalo*.
This variation on an accepted theme, the traditional aversion of soldiers to marriage, has points in common with *The Bold Grenadier* (No. 17) and *The Sentry* (No. 92).

23 *The Cuckoo*

A

A walking and a talking
And a walking goes I
For to meet my Sweet William
He will come by and bye

For to meet him it's pleasure
And to part it is grief
For a false hearted young man
He's worse than a thief

I do wish I was a scholar
I could handle to my pen
There is one private letter
To my true Love I would send

I would send and let you know my love
Of my sorrow grief and woe
May the blessing attend
On the road where you may go.

O the cuckoo she is a fine bird
She do sing as she fly
She bring to us good tidings
And tell to us no lie

She sucks the white flowers
To keep her voice clear
And the more sings cuckoo
The summer is drawing near

THE CUCKOO
B

The Americans have stole my true love away
And I in old. England no longer can stay
I will cross the briny ocean all on my soft heart
To find out the true love whom I do love best

And when I have found out my joy and delight
I'll be constant unto him by day and by night
I will always prove as constant as a true turtle dove
And I never will in no time prove false to my love

For meeting is a pleasure a courting it is a grief
He's a false hearted young man he will bring you to grave
O the grave it will moulder you and bring you to the dust
Scarce one man out of twenty pretty maidens can you trust

Come all you pretty maidens wherever you be
Don't settle your mind on your sycamore tree
For the leaves they will but wither and the branches will die
And you'll be forsaken, you know not for why.

The cuckoo is a merry bird she sings as she flies
She bring to us good tidings and tell to us no lies
She sucks little birds' eggs to make her sing clear
But she'll ever sing cuckoo till the summer draws near

A
[679 John Holt at Hazelbury Plucknett 1905
1479 Mrs Elizabeth Smitherd (65) at Tewkesbury 1908]
First two stanzas from 1479, remainder from 679

  6.4 *near*: old form of comparative (nigher).
  1479 adds a final stanza:
    So if he's gone let him go, let him sink or let him swim
    For he's sadly mistaken if he thinks that I mourn
This incongruous accretion is clearly from a different source.

B
[679 (see above)
1521 Robert Rowlands at Shipley 1908]
  (Six other English versions, of which four are mere fragments. Eight American versions.)

THE CUCKOO

With the exception of stanza 3, which is from 679, all the stanzas are from 1521.

1.3 should evidently end with 'breast', not 'heart', but in any case the line is confused.
3.1 *For meeting*: 679 To meet her
a courting: evidently a corruption of 'parting'.
4.2 *on your sycamore tree*: 1472 on the top of a tree

Sharp published in *Folk Songs from Somerset*, III, 1906, and *English Folk Songs*, Selected Edition, Vol. I, 1921, a text of this song similar to A. Versions were noted by several collectors, and it was evidently of wide popularity. The versions are far from unanimous, and it is impossible to trace a single prototype. The theme of all is the cuckoo as the type of fickleness in men.

The lines relating to the cuckoo are often printed separately as a song for children or as a nursery rhyme (e.g. by Halliwell, 1842).

I have assembled two texts from elements in three of Sharp's versions, since none by itself is complete. For the sake of metrical consistency I have, where necessary, printed stanzas of two four-foot lines as four two-foot lines, and *vice versa*.

24 Dabbling in the Dew

Where shall I meet you my pretty little dear
    With your red rosy cheeks and your coal black hair
I'm going a milking kind sir she answered me
    But it's dabbling in the dew where you might find me

Shall I carry your pail then my pretty little dear
O no sir O no sir I'll carry it myself

Suppose I was to kiss you my pretty little dear
That would be no harm sir she answered me

Suppose I was to throw you down my pretty little dear
So you must help me up again kind sir she answered me

Suppose you're in the family way my pretty little dear
You'll have to stand the father of it sir she answered me

Suppose I was to run away my pretty little dear
Then I must run the faster kind sir she answered me

Suppose I was to run too fast my pretty little dear
O the divil would fitch you back again sir she answered me

[569 John Swain, Christmas Day 1909. Two other versions]
The ms. is very irregular, and in order to make a readable version, I have emended it thus:

    1 as in 569. (It is clear from the musical texts that lines 2 and 4 are sung as refrain-lines in every stanza.)
    2 569 Shall I carry your pail then my pretty little dear ...
        O no sir O no sir I'd rather go myself
        ... I'll carry it myself
    3 Ms. contains, between the two lines printed above, a defective line, thus:
        ... do something...
    7.2 *fitch you*: 569 fitch me

Otherwise 4–7 as in ms., except that the phrases 'my pretty little dear' and '(kind) sir she answered me' have been added.

Sharp first printed this in *Folk Songs from Somerset*, II, 1905, with the following note on the words: 'They are quite unsuitable for publication, so Mr Marson has rewritten the ballad, retaining the first verse only and the refrain.' Marson's insipid text was indeed so remote from the original song that in *English Folk Songs*, Selected Edition, 1921, Vol. I, Sharp abandoned it and printed a text based largely on that given in Halliwell's *Nursery Rhymes of England* (1842). He says: 'This is a very popular song all over England, and I have taken down a large number of variants. The traditional words, which vary but little, are very free and unconventional.' Other printed texts, however, e.g. those in the *Journal of the Folk-Song Society*, No. 17, 1913, are not at all 'free and unconventional' in this sense. They show considerable variation, implying some editorial ingenuity on the part of collectors.

'Dabbling' is varied by 'roving' and 'rolling'.

25 The Dandy Man

Oh one day I was taken very ill
He went to buy a couple of fowls
He bought a couple I do declare
A magpie and an owl

So women all take my advice
And mark what I do say
If you should wed with a dandy man
You will have to rue the day

He put them in the pot to boil
Tied up in a dirty cloth
He boiled them up, both feathers, guts and all
And swore 'twas Jamon's broth

Chorus

Oh every night while in bed
Like an elephant he lies
He never takes his breeches off
He sleeps in women's stays

Chorus

[142 William Nott at Meshaw 1904. No other version.]

2.4 *have*:? live

By the middle of the nineteenth century the word 'dandy' meant merely a fop; previously 'dandies wore stays, studied femininity, and tried to undo their manhood. Lord Petersham headed them.' Camden Hotten, *The Slang Dictionary*, 1864. Lord Petersham, who nourished in 1812, gave his name to a kind of corded silk ribbon still in use.

26 *The Derby Ram*

As I was going to Derby
Upon a market day
I saw the finest ram sir
That ever was fed on hay
    And indeed sir 'tis true sir
    I never was given to lie
    And if you had been in Derby
    You'd have seen it as well as I

This ram was fat behind sir
This ram was fat before
And under his pretty legs sir
You could drive a coach and four

The space between his hams sir
Was forty yards complete
And a gallery there was built sir
Where the Quakers used to meet

The wool that grew on his back sir
It grew mountains high
And the eagles built their nest sir
For I heard the young ones cry

The wool that grew on its tail sir
It covered five acres of ground
And the fleece was sold in London
For forty thousand pound

The butcher that killed this ram sir
Was drowned in his blood
And forty thousand more sir
Were carried away with the flood

THE DERBY RAM

[1955 Sister Emma (71) at Clewer 1909. Three other English and American versions]

The following additional stanzas occur in 496 John Durbin 1904:

> The wool that growed on his belly would reach unto the ground
> And that was carried to Derby and sold for a thousand pound
> The tail that growed on his behind was threescore yards and an ell
> And he was took to Derby to toll the market bell

Many different versions of this song have been noted by collectors. Apparently a simple piece of nonsense of the 'tall story' variety, it is in reality part of a primitive purification ritual, which was performed in the north Midlands until fifty years ago. The ram, commonly called 'the old tup', was constructed like the hobby-horse of other regions. A real or partly real sheep's head was mounted on a pole to which a sheepskin or sack was attached, concealing the performer who represented the ram. A company of half a dozen went round houses and farms performing the song, with suitable actions, at Christmas time or the New Year. Apart from 'the old tup' the company consisted of some of the following: the butcher, a boy with a basin, Little Devil Doubt, a clown with a black face, an old man, an old woman, and the collector. The ceremony is connected with the idea of expiating the unconfessed sins of the community with the blood of a scapegoat.

The Oxford Dictionary of Nursery Rhymes (1951) contains an eight-stanza version and further information about earlier texts.

27 *The Devil's in the Girl*

It's of a lusty gentleman
Returning from his play
He knocked at his true love's door
That night with her to stay
She quickly let this young man in
And called him her delight
Saying take me in your arms my love
And bide till morning light

The maid she was a crafty jade
And to her love did say
Oh what did please you best my love
While you were at the play
He says, my dear I learnt a tune
Forget I never shall
It's called a very pretty tune,
The devil's in the girl.

Oh kind sir let me hear that tune
If you your pipes can play
I'll listen with attention
So now play up I pray
Oh the tune it is so beautiful
And pleases me so well
All night I'll lay, if you will play
The devil's in the girl.

The sound awoke her mother
All on the second floor
Who ran out with her bedgown on
And like a bull did roar
She spoiled this young man's music
And pummelled him as well
This jade she said, he played the tune
The devil's in the girl.

THE DEVIL'S IN THE GIRL

This young man quickly left them
His journey to pursue
But mark what followed after
This young girl poorly grew
Her mother said one morning
Oh what's the matter Sal
You mope about just like a goose
The devil's in the girl.

Six months it soon passed over
Her gown it wouldn't meet
Her mother finding out the same
She said It is a treat
Oh daughter, said the mother
The music makes you swell
Why it's never good to play the tune
The devil's in the girl.

Twelve months it soon passed over
This young man out of fun
He went that way and met the maid
Who had a lovely son
She said Kind Sir, come, marry me
For you can please me well
He smiled and shook his head and said
The devil's in the girl.

Oh if I played the tune
It pleased you no doubt
You ought to pay the piper
If he the tune played out
So you may go your way fair maid
I cannot be your pal
You can get some other one to play
The devil's in the girl.

[196 William Natt at Meshaw 1904. No other version]

The sexual symbolism in the playing of pipes occurs also in No. 35, *The German Flute*.

28 *Down by a River Side*

As I walked out one May morning
Down by the river side
I heard a couple discoursing
Which filled my heart with pride

Come sing to me another song
And my bride you shall be
Kind sir she said I'm yet too young
Your bride for to be

The younger you are the better for me
The fitter to be my bride
And perhaps that I might say some day
I married my wife a maid.

He kissed her and he courted her
Till he gained the will of her
And as soon as he gained the will of her
He stoled her maidenhead

The grass was wet and slippery
And both her feet did slide
They both fell down together
Down by the riverside.

Since you have had your will of me
Pray tell to me your name
That when my pretty babe is born
I may call it the same

My name is Captain Thunderbolt
To you I'll never marry
I met the glazier's daughter dear
Down by the river side.

This is not what you promised me
Down by the river side
You promised that you'd marry me
Make me your lawful Bride.

DOWN BY A RIVER SIDE

If I promised that I'd marry you
'Tis more than I would do
For I never intended to wed a girl
So easy found as you.

It's other farmers' daughters
To market they may go
While I poor girl must stop at home
And rock the cradle o'er.

And rock the cradle o'er and o'er
And sing sweet lullaby
Was there ever poor girl in all the Town
So crossed in love as I?

[427 Mrs Overd 1904. Five other English and two American versions]
  7.1 *Captain Thunderbolt*: supposedly the devil.
  7.3 *glazier*: probably 'grazier' is meant, but for the interchangeable 'l' and 'r' compare No. 4, *The American Stranger*, in which 'royal' for 'loyal' occurs.
 10.1 *It's other farmers' daughters*: 427 It's of the farmer's daughter
[1071 (Richard Adams, 77, 1906) contains the following additional stanzas:
O the younger you are my dear
The better you are for me
He took her by the lily white hand
And kissed both cheek and chin
He took her to his marriage room
To sleep all night with him

The forepart of the night how they did sport and play
She slept in his arms till day

Go down in your father's garden
Sit down and cry your fill
And when you think on what you done
You'll blame your own good will

She said there's a herb in my uncle's garden
And some do call it rue
When fishes fly like swallows do
Young men they will prove true]

29 *No my Love not I*

As I walked out one morning all in the month of May
There I spied a fair pretty maid, a gathering of sweet hay
I asked her if she'd wed with me, I'd marry her by and by
But the answer that she gave to me, not I my love, not I.

Two or three months came after this and then
This pretty fair damsel growed thicker round her waist
Her gown it would not join, my boys, her apron strings w'nt tie
And she cursed the very hour when she said, no my love not I.

She wrote a letter unto him to come immediately
But the answer he returned again, not I my love, not I.
Supposing I should come to you, shouldn't I be much to blame
My parents would be angry they'd laugh at my disdain

To think that you're so very low, and I'm so very high
Do you think that I could marry you, not I my love not I.

The best thing that I can advise you for to do
Is to take your baby on your back and a begging for to go
And when that you are weary love, you may sit down and cry
And curse the very hour that you said no my love not I.

And when that you are weary love, you may sit down and cry
And curse the very hour that you said, no my love, not I.

[473 Mrs Overd's words 1904]

Related in theme but not in form to *Down by a River Side*.
    2.1 Line defective.
    3.4 *disdain*: i.e. the fact that she had disdained him before.

30 *I'm a Day too Young*

As I walked out one May morning
One May morning so early
Who should I spy but a fair pretty maid
Come tippling over the plains to me
    With my fil fol lol and the diddle all the day
    With my fil fol lol and the diddle all the day

I asked this maid how old she was
I asked her again how old she was
I'm a day too young to be your bride
I'm a day too young to lay by thy side

I took her by the middle so small
And gently laid her on the ground
I served her so but once or twice
And I found she was not a day too young

Now you have had your will of me
And robbed me of my sweet liberty
I pray young man pray tell to me
When my wedding day shall be

My wedding day never troubles me
For I never intend to married be
You may lie and you may brew
And drink your ale while it is new

And carry your big belly home to your mam
And tell her you're just one day too young

[747 John Vincent at Priddy 1905. No other version]
Related in theme but not in form to the two foregoing.

31 *Down in my Garden*

Down in my garden there grows a fine flower
A flower that is seen at the spring time of the year
Where I and my lover spent many long hours
'Twas kissing and courting but never was too near

There's one thing more I will ask of a favour
Hoping that you will grant it unto me
That's one night more to sleep with my mother
And all my life afterwards I'll sleep along with thee

O yes! O yes! that is already granted
And sighing and crying they all went to bed
'Twas early next morning this young man awakened
This young man awakened and found his wife dead

It is for your sweet sake I'll be a widow man for ever
If I should wed, luck it shall be forsaken
So fare thee away my love
And come along with me.

[375 Lucy White 1904. No other version]
Printed in *The Journal of the Folk-Song Society*, No. 31, 1927

32 *The Female Cabin Boy*

'Tis of a pretty female as you shall understand
She had a mind of roving into some foreign land
Attired in sailor's clothing she boldly did appear
And engaged with the captain to serve him for one year.

She engaged with the captain as cabin boy to be
The wind it was in favour, and so they put to sea.
The captain's lady being on board she seemed for to enjoy,
And glad the captain had engaged with a female cabin boy.

THE FEMALE CABIN BOY

So nimble was this pretty girl she did her duty well
Only mark what follows after, the song it soon will tell
By eating the captain's biscuits her colour did destroy
And the waist did swell of pretty Nell the female cabin boy

One night among the sailors there was a pretty row
(*line missing*)
They bundled from their hammocks which did their rest destroy
They swore about the groaning of the female cabin boy

O doctor, O doctor, the cabin boy did cry
The sailors swear by all and one the cabin boy will die
The doctor ran with all his might a-smiling at the fun
To think a sailor lad could have a daughter or a son.

O when the sailors heard the joke they all began to stare
The child belonged to none of them they solemnly declared
The lady to the captain said I wish you joy
'Twas you or either I betrayed the female cabin boy

[782 Susan Williams at Haselbury Plucknett 1905]

33 *The Foggy Dew*

When I was young and in my prime
I carried on the weaving trade
And all the harm that ever I done
Was courting a fair pretty maid

I courted her one midsummer day
And part of the winter too
Till I thought it my time to roll her in my arms
Think no more on the foggy foggy dew.

THE FOGGY DEW

One night as I lay on my bed
As I lay fast asleep
Then up came this pretty fair maid
And most bitterly did weep

She wept she moaned she tore her hair
Crying Alas what shall I do,
This night I'm resolved to stay with you
For fear of the foggy dew.

'Twas in the first part of the night
We passed our time away
And in the later part of the night
For she stayed with me till day

And when she rose and saw the light
She cries I am undone
I said fair maid be not afraid
For the foggy dew is gone

O when shall you come on my dear
O when shall you come on
When oaken leaves fall off the trees
And greener ones come on

O that will be too long my dear
O that will be too long
My heart will burst, and die I must
That is if you don't come on

The very next day I married her
I married her for life
And ever since I married her
I proved her for my wife

When we have a child my dear
O that will make you smile
And when we have another
We will wait a little while

THE FOGGY DEW

And when we have another my dear
And have another too
Why we must leave off kissing
And think on the foggy dew

And I never told her of her faults
And I never do intend so to do
But every time she smiles at me
I think of the foggy dew

[87 Lucy White and Louie Hooper 1903
107 No source given
297 John Voke at Castle of Comfort 1904
1891 William Stokes at Chew Stoke 1908]
   (One other fragmentary English version, and one American)

This is a composite version using lines and stanzas from the four ms. versions enumerated above. Minor emendations are given below. For a full discussion, including the ms. versions complete, see Introduction, pp. 45–57.

    4.3 *This night I'm resolved*: 1891 This I'm resolved

The above emendation is substantiated by the broadside text in *The Common Muse* (Pinto and Rodway, 1957), No. cxciii.

    6.4 *gone*: 107 done
    7.1 *shall you*: 107 you shall
    7.1 *come on*: marry me.
    7 and 8 In this dialogue the girl speaks first.
    9.4 *proved*: approved

34 *Gently Johnny my Jingalo*

I put my hand all on her toe
    Fair maid is a lily O
I put my hand all on her toe
She says to me do you want to go?
    Come to me quietly
    Do not do no injury
    Gently Johnny my jingalo.

GENTLY JOHNNY MY JINGALO

I put my hand all on her knee
She says to me do you want to see?

I put my hand all on her thigh
She says to me do you want to try?

I put my hand all on her billy
She says to me do you want to fill'ee?

I put my hand all on her breast
She says to me do you want a kiss?

I put my hand all on her head
She says you want my maidenhead.

[1176 William Tucker at Ashcott 1907. One other fragmentary version]

Sharp printed an entirely re-written text of this song, appending the following note (*Folk Songs from Somerset*, 1904–9): 'I know nothing of this song. I have never heard anyone sing it except Mr Tucker; nor do I know of any broadside or any published folk-song with which it has any connection. Mr Tucker told me that he learned the song from his father, who always declared it to be his favourite song.

'The words as I took them down were too coarse for publication. I have, however, been able to re-write the first and third lines of every verse without, I think, wholly sacrificing the character of the original song. The lines that recur in each verse run very smoothly and prettily and seem to suggest that the song is of some antiquity.'

He reprinted this text in *English Folk Songs*, Selected Edition, Vol. I (1921) with a similar note, adding: 'I have no doubt but that it is a genuine folk-song.'

I have discovered no other printed text. A writer in the *Journal of the Folk-Song Society*, No. 20, 1916, suggests that the refrain is a corruption of 'Gentil joli jongleur', and refers to the refrain of a medieval lyric in *Early English Lyrics*, No. CL (Chambers & Sidgwick):

Draw me nere, draw me nere
Draw me nere, ye jolly juggelere!

The writer adds that the song 'appears to be a relic of an old minstrel song'.
In the middle ages jugglers were notorious for promiscuity and craftiness. Cf. Chaucer, *Friar's Tale*, 1.1467:

A lousy jogelour can deceyve thee.

35 The German Flute

O it's on the banks of roses where my love and I sit down
He pulled out his German flute and he played to her a tune
In the middle of the tune O she sigh and she sing
Lovely Johnny dearest Johnny do not leave me

When I was but a little one I used to hear my mother say
She would rather see me dead and laid in cold clay
And I should get tied up to any runaway
I'll get roving with you Johnny in the morning

Indeed I am no runaway and that you may very well know
I can drink a glass of beer and I can leave it alone
If your mother do not like me she must keep you at home
That I mean to be married in the morning

Fare you well father, fare you well mother
Fare you well sister likewise my youngest brother
Yes I am going to forsake you all for the lad I love so dear
And I means to be married in the morning

[1226 Susie Clacker per Jack Barnard at Bridgwater 1907. No other version]

36 Good Old Man

O where are you going to my good old man
O where are you going? and she called him her lamb
O where are you going my loving husband
You're the best old man that's alive alive alive
You're the best old man that's alive.

Going to the alehouse you old bitch
Alive alive alive, you're the best old man that's alive.

GOOD OLD MAN

O where are you going to my good old man
O where are you going? and she called him her lamb
O where are you going my loving husband
You're the best old man that's alive alive alive
You're the best old man that's alive.

Going to get drunk you old Queen
Alive alive alive, you're the best old man that's alive.

O what will you have for supper my good old man
O what will you have for supper? and she called him her lamb
O what will you have for supper my loving husband
You're the best old man that's alive alive alive
You're the best old man that's alive

Eggs and bacon you old Queen
Alive alive alive, you're the best old man that's alive.

How many will you have my good old man
How many will you have? and she called him her lamb
How many will you have my loving husband
You're the best old man that's alive alive alive
You're the best old man that's alive.

Three dozen eggs and two pounds of bacon you old Dear
Alive alive alive, you're the best old man that's alive

So many they will kill you my good old man
So many they will kill you, and she called him her lamb
So many they will kill you my loving husband
You're the best old man that's alive alive alive
You're the best old man that's alive

Then I shall die my old dear
Alive alive alive, you're the best old man that's alive.

Where will you be buried to, my good old man
Where will you be buried to? and she called him her lamb
Where will you be buried to my loving husband
You're the best old man that's alive alive alive
You're the best old man that's alive.

GOOD OLD MAN

In a dunghill you old Queen
Alive alive alive, you're the best old man that's alive.

What will you be buried there for, my good old man
What will you be buried there for? and she called him her lamb
What will you be buried there for my loving husband
You're the best old man that's alive alive alive
You're the best old man that's alive.

Let all old rubbish go together woman.
Alive alive alive, you're the best old man that's alive.

[2047 Captain Lewis at Minehead 1909. No other version]

The ms. omits the repeated lines, and indicates that the old man's replies ('Going to the alehouse', etc.) were spoken, not sung.

    1.6 *bitch: ms. has* b—h (or Queen or dear or witch)

37 *Gossip Joan*

A

Good morning Gossip Joan
Where are you going a walking
I'm going in a he he, a he he, a he he
And a belly full of drink
O God save Joan

Now my old hen she got a brood
Just under a hackney saddle
And there she sat for a fifteen weeks, a fifteen
    weeks, a fifteen weeks
Till all her eggs were addled
O God save Joan

GOSSIP JOAN

Now my old colly cow she's a calved
Just under the parlour window
If it hadn't a been for a bull bull bull, a bull
    bull bull, a bull bull bull
She wouldn't have had her labour
O God save Joan

B

He sat my hen a-brood
Upon a hackney saddle
And she never brought out no che wee wee, *etc.*
Because her eggs was addle.
God save Joan!

Old Zow she eat the trough
And was not that a wonder?
Instead of her little che wee wee, *etc*
She brought forth nothing but timber
God save Joan!

Old owl flied out of the barn
And was not that a wonder?
If I'd have been a little bit soo-oo-oo-oo-*ner*
I might have catched him!
God save Joan!

[A 1750 Charles Ash at Crowcombe 1908
B 28 John Gillard at Hambridge 1903]
   (One other fragmentary version)

A
   3.1 *colly*: black.

B
   3.3 *soo-oo-oo-oo-ner*: possibly in imitation of the owl.

Versions of this song were popular at least from the time of the Restoration (see Thomas Durfey, *Pills to Purge Melancholy*, 1661). Words similar to, but not identical with these have been printed, e.g. in Alfred Williams, *Folk Songs of the Upper Thames*, 1923.

38 *Hares on the Mountains*

A

Young women they'll run like hares on the mountains
Young women they'll run like hares on the mountains
If I was but a young man I'd soon go a-hunting
To my right fol diddle dero, to my right fol diddle dee.

Young women they sing like birds in the bushes
Young women they sing like birds in the bushes
If I was a young man I'd go and bang the bushes
To my right fol diddle dero, to my right fol diddle dee.

Young women they'll swim like ducks in the water
Young women they'll swim like ducks in the water
If I was a young man I'd go and swim all after
To my right fol diddle dero, to my right fol diddle dee.

B

If all those young men were as rushes a growing
Then all those pretty maidens will get scythes go a mowing
                                        Fal lal etc.

If all those young men were as hares on the mountains
Then all those pretty maidens will get guns go a hunting

If all those young men were as ducks in the water
Then all those pretty maidens would soon follow after

C

Sally my dear shall I come to bed to you (*bis*)
She laugh and reply I'm afraid you'll undo me
Sing fal the diddle ido
Sing whack fal the diddle day.

O Sally my dear why I will not undo you (*bis*)
She laugh and reply you may come to bed to me

Sally my dear I cannot undo my breeches (*bis*)
She laugh and reply take a knife and rip stitches

O Sally my dear I cannot undo them (*bis*)
She laugh and reply there's a knife in the window

HARES ON THE MOUNTAINS

Now he took off his breeches and into bed tumbled (*bis*)
I leave you to guess how the young couple fumbled

If blackbirds was blackbirds as thrushes was thrushes (*bis*)
How soon the young men would go beating the bushes

Should young women be hares and race round the mountain (*bis*)
Young men' d take guns and they'd soon go a hunting

Should young women be ducks and should swim round the ocean (*bis*)
Young men would turn drakes and soon follow after

D

If young women could build like Blackbirds and Thrushes
There's many a young man would soon find out the nestes

If young women could swim like fishes in water
There's many a young man would strip and swim after

If young women could fly like birds in the air
There's many a young man could cock and let fire.

[A 16 Louie Hooper and Lucy White 1903
B 351 Mrs Lock at Muchelney 1904
C 960 John Barnett at Bridgwater 1906
D 1131 William Davis at Porlock Weir 1906]
(No other versions)

The latter two of these versions are given under the title *Sally my Dear*. Sharp published *Hares on the Mountains* in the *Journal of the Folk-Song Society*, No. 6, 1905, in *Folk Songs from Somerset*, iii, 1906, and in *English Folk Songs*, Selected Edition, 1921, Vol. I. He also printed *Sally my Dear in English Folk Songs*, Selected Edition, 1921, Vol. II, with an entirely re-written text of Stanzas 1–5 of C, adding the following note: 'The words of the first three stanzas had, of necessity, to be somewhat altered.' He thus treats *Sally my Dear* as an integral part of *Hares on the Mountains*,

Stanzas 1–5 of C may be a comedy of sexual impotence; 'fumble' (C 5.2) means 'to fondle or caress', but 'fumbler' and 'fumbling' imply impotence.

Another song containing the idea of a girl evading pursuit by undergoing a scries of animal metamorphoses is *The Two Magicians*. Hares are notoriously wild in the mating season. Witches were able to transform themselves into hares. The sexual implications of 'blackbirds and thrushes' are the subject of another song, *Three Maids a Milking*, No. 102.

39 A Harvest Song

Who knocks there?
Poor Peg.
What's poor Peg want?
A shroud to wrap poor Tom in.
What's poor Tom dead?
Yes.
When did er die?
Yesterday in the morning gray
Parted poor Tom and I
I heard a bird singing in the wood
Poor Tom was like to die
Now what shall us do
For poor Tom's sake
For he was a right honest man
We'll take this cup and drink him up
And so shall everyone
Ring a right and do no wrong.
Poor Tom is dead and gone
Boom (*drink*) Boom (*drink*) Boom (*drink*)

[2019 William Shepherd (93) at Winchcomb Workhouse 1909. No other version]

'He said this was often done at Harvest Home. One man knocked the floor with his stick whereupon the above dialogue took place. The last few lines were sung to a major version of "The Miller of Dee". Then they all said Boom (to represent a bell) then a deep pull at their glasses. This repeated three times.' (Sharp's note.)
    Travelling in England between 1679 and 1683, Oliger Jacobaeus, a Dane, wrote down in phonetic English a version of this song which he heard in London:
    'Who is there? Poor maid full of sorre and care. Whad will poor maid have? I beseech to rep poor Tham in. Is poor Tham dead? Poor Tham is dead. When did poor Tham dey? Yesterday in the morning grey. Partit poor Tham, and deid, deid, deid. I heared a bort sing in the wood, poor Tham is dead, we will drink a half for poor Tham's sake, for he was a right anish man. I will drink a half w'play for me self w'so schall every man. Sup, pru, nel, mel, dal, Yohn' (? Sue, Prue, Nell, Moll, Doll, Joan). (See *Journal of the Folk-Song Society*, No. 5, 1904.)

A HARVEST SONG

It has been suggested that this is a secret Royalist drinking song, 'poor Tom' being Charles I. In any case it is evidently related to the well-known round:

> Let's have a peal for John Cook's soul,
> For he was a very, very honest man.

40 *Haymaking Courtship*

A soldier walked in the field one day
To view the flowers that grew so gay
He saw a fair maid stripped in her shirt
As she was raking round yonder hay

He says fair maid lay down your rake
And go with me to yonder wake
Now I dare not leave my master's hay
He'll stop my wages turn me away

He followed her from field to field
With great persuading got her to yield
She put on her gown threw down her rake
And went with the soldier to yonder wake

And when they came to yonder wake
He entreated her with ale wine and cake
He bought her rings jewels and gloves
And so he gained the fair maid's love

When twenty weeks were come and passed
This fair maid grew pale at last
Then she curst the hour all in the day
She went with the soldier and left the hay

When forty weeks were come and gone
This lovely damsel brought forth a son
Then she blest the hour all in the day
She went with the soldier and left the hay

HAYMAKING COURTSHIP

When the soldier this news did know
Great favour unto this girl did show
They married were and she blessed the day
She went with the soldier and left the hay

[519 Mr Palmer 1904. One other version and a fragment]
  2.2 *wake*: 519 rake
  3.3–4.2 1053 Mrs Elizabeth Loveless (49) at Stolford 1906
    She put down her rake and put on her gown
    As she marched with the soldier across the barren ground
    He took her up into an inn
    Where he treated her to both wine and gin
  6 1053
    When forty weeks had gone and passed
    Her cherry cheeks grew pale at last
    It made pretty maidens sigh and say
    Cursed be the hour that I left my master's hay
This is the final stanza in 1053.
  For a similar instance of a girl's alternately cursing and blessing her association with a soldier, compare *Cold Blow and a Rainy Night* (No. 22).

41 *The Hazelbury Girl*

As I was going to Hazelbury
'Twas on a market day
There came a little Hazelbury girl
A -jogging along my way
Her business was to market
With butter and cheese and eggs
So we both jogged on together my boys
Sing fal the dal diddle all day

We jogged along together
Together side by side
This pretty little Hazelbury girl
Her garter came untied
And for fear that she might lose it
I unto her did say
Your garter is untied my love
Sing fal the dal diddle all day.

THE HAZELBURY GIRL

Oh now you've been so venturesome
So venturesome and free
Oh now you've been so venturesome
Will you tie it up for me?
Oh yes, oh yes if you come
To the undergrove
So we both jogged on together my boys
Sing fal the dal diddle all day.

I took her to the undergrove
The grass grew very high
I laid the pretty girl on her back
Her garter for to tie
And was tying up her garter
Such sights as I never did see
So we both jogged on together my boys
Sing fal the dal diddle all day.

Oh now you've had your will of me
Pray tell to me your name
Likewise your occupation
From where and whence you came.
My name is Johnny the Rover
From Dublin town I came
And I live alongside of the Ups and Downs
Sing fal the dal diddle all day.

So when she came to Hazelbury
Her butter was not sold
By losing of her fortune
Which made her blood run cold.
He's gone he's gone he's gone
He's not the lad for me
For he lives alongside of the Ups and Downs
Sing fal the dal diddle all day.

[57 Tom Lymes at Bredon, Packington 1903. One other incomplete version]

4.7 *jogged*: 'jog' (like 'diddle' in the refrain) can mean 'fornicate'.
5.7 *the Ups and Downs*: (57 ups and downs) the 69th Foot Regiment, so nicknamed perhaps because '69' reads the same when it is upside

down. Until it became the 2nd Battalion of the Welsh Regiment, in about 1881, this was a mixed force of old crocks and young recruits who at one time served as marines. Hence the elusiveness of the young man in the song.

42 *Hecketty Pecketty*

Hecketty Pecketty needles and pins
Matrimony and sorrow begins
A maid I am and a maid I'll die
Man's love to me is all my eye.
Think I'll bide home to wash and brew
To mend his holes in his stockings too
While he is out to pub-e-lic house
And Heaven be praised I've found him out
Fol de lol, lol de lol, li di o.

[450 Mrs Hooper at Hambridge 1904. No other version]

line 4 *my eye*: this expression for 'nonsense' goes back to the late eighteenth century at least

43 *High Germany*

O Polly my dear Polly the rout has now begun
And we must march away by the beating of the drum
Go dress yourself all in your best and come along with me
I'll take you to the war my love in the Isle of Germany

O Billy my dear Billy listen to what I say
My feet they are so very sore I cannot march away
Besides my dearest Billy I am with child by thee
I'm not fitting for the war, my love, in the Isle of Germany

I'll buy you a horse my love, my Polly you shall ride
And all my delight shall be a walking by your side
We'll call to every ale house that ever we pass by
We'll sweetheart on the road my love, get married by and bye

HIGH GERMANY

Cruel, cruel was the war when first the rout began
And out of Old England went many a smart young man
They pressed my Love away from me likewise my brothers three
They sent them to the war my love in the Isle of Germany

The drum that my love's beating is covered with green
The pretty lambs is sporting 'tis pleasure to be seen
And when my pretty babe is born sits smiling on my knee
I'll think upon my own true love in the Isle of Germany

[878 Mrs Overd at Langport 1906. Three other versions and one fragment]
1361 William Stokes at Chew Stoke 1907

  1.1 *the rout has now begun*: marching orders have been given.
  1.4 1361 And I'll take you to the wars that's in High Germany
  2.2 1361 My feet they are so tender I cannot march away
  4.2 *smart*: 1361 bright
  5 1361
    It grieved my heart sore to lose my brothers three
    It grieved me much more to lose my dear Billy
    For when I nursed my baby upon my bended knees
    It caused me to curse all the wars that's in High Germany

This version of one of the best of folk songs has not previously been published. Sharp printed in the *Journal of the Folk-Song Society*, No. 6, 1905, and again in *English Folk Songs*, Selected Edition, 1921, Vol. I, a text 'compiled from different versions'. In this there is no mention of the theme of extra-marital pregnancy, and the words 'with child by' (2.3) are replaced by 'in love with', as sung by at least one of Sharp's singers. However, this clearly enfeebles the sense.

44 *I'm Seventeen Come Sunday*

    As I walked out one May morning
    One May morning so early
    I overtook a handsome maid
    Just as the sun was a-rising.
        With my ree rum a day
        Fal the diddle i day
        Fal the dol the diddle-i-day

I'M SEVENTEEN COME SUNDAY

Her shoes were bright and her stockings white
And her buckles shone like silver
She had a black and a roving eye
And her hair hung over her shoulder

How old are you my fair pretty maid
How old are you my honey
She answered me, quite cheerfully
I am seventeen, come Sunday

Will you marry me my fair pretty maid
Will you marry me, my honey?
She answered me quite cheerfully
I dare not, for my Mammy

If you'll come unto my Mammy's house
When the moon is shining brightly
I will come down and let you in
And my Mammy shall not hear me

I went unto her Mammy's house
When the moon was shining brightly
She did come down and let me in
And I laid in her arms till morning

Now soldier will you marry me
Now is your time, or never
For if you do not marry me
I am undone for ever

And now she is the soldier's wife
And the soldier loves her dearly
The drum and fife is her delight
And a merry man in the morning

[225 William Spearing at lie Bruers 1904. Two other versions, one fragmentary]

    8.3 *her*: 225 gives both *her* and *my* bracketed.
    8.4 This line is from another of Sharp's versions: 225 gives *And a merry old man is mine O*. 'Merry' means 'amorously inclined, willing'.

I'M SEVENTEEN COME SUNDAY

The original of this song, whatever it was, shocked all the editors, from the eighteenth century onwards, into a frenzy of emendation—so much so that I cannot believe the above is the original, though it is probably nearer than anything hitherto published. Sharp reprinted this text in the *Journal of the Folk-Song Society*, No. 6, 1905, silently replacing 6.4 by 'And I stayed with her till morning'. The text he published in *English Folk Songs*, Selected Edition, 1921, Vol. I, is taken from a broadside, and omits stanza 6 altogether.

Baring-Gould published in *Songs of the West*, 1890-1905, a text almost entirely composed by his collaborator H. Fleetwood Sheppard, appending the following note: 'For good reasons we could not give the words as taken down.' He then cites editors from Burns onward, all of whom, 'for several reasons', emended the stanzas they considered offensive.

Some printed versions give 'Will you take a man' for 'Will you marry me'.

45 *I Sowed some Seeds*

A landlord had one daughter
And a nice young girl too she was
Above her garters I dare not go
I being a stranger I fell in danger
For doing so, for doing so

I sowed some seed, all in some grove
All in some grove, there grows no green
Now for to repeat, I could not stir
I being a stranger I fell in danger
For doing so, for doing so

When nine long months was gone and past
This pretty girl had a fine son at last
Now she must keep it and call it her own
And reap the seed that I have sown
For doing so, for doing so

[290 Lucy White at Hambridge 1904, who had the second and third stanzas from Susan Woodland, over 40 years dead. No other version]

46 *I've been a Roving*

I've been a roving, I've been a roving
To the ale house and the buts
I am coming I am coming
With my liquor in my guts

I've been a roving, I've been a roving
Where the honeysuckle creep
I am coming I am coming
With the roses on my cheeks.

I've been a roving, I've been a roving
To the Noble and Cock Hen
I am coming, I am coming
To my bairn back again

[1450 Jack Barnard at Bridgwater 1908. No other version]
3.4 *bairn*: ? barn

47 *I Wish I had never Known*

I wish I had never known no man at all
Since love has been a grief and has proved my downfall
Since love has been a grief and a tyrant to me
I lost my love fighting for sweet liberty

I wish I had never seen his curled hair
And neither that I'd been in his company there
'Twas his red rosy cheeks his dark rolling eye
And his flattering tongue caused my poor heart to sigh

People came to me and thus they did say
Your lover has gone has gone far away
But if ever he return I will crown him with joy
I fly to the arms of my dear darling boy.

I WISH I HAD NEVER KNOWN

If I had wings like an eagle I'd fly
I'd fly to the arms of my dear darling boy
And on his soft bosom I'd build up my nest
I'd lay my head down on his white snowy breast

Some say I'm with child but that I'll deny
Some say I'm with child but I'll prove it a lie
I'll tarry awhile and soon let them know
That he likes me too well to serve me so.

Well some do wear spencers and I don't wear none
And they that don't let me can leave me alone
He'll have me or leave me and so let me go
For I don't care a straw if he have me or no

[401 Mrs Overd 1904. No other version]
   5.2 *I'm*: 401 I

In view of some inconsistencies of attitude on the part of the girl, it must be supposed that this text is incomplete or confused; but I have not been able to discover a more consistent 'Original'. The song is distantly related to *The Blackbird* (*Songs from the Countryside*, Collinson and Dillon, 1946).

48 *The Irish Girl*

As I walked out one morning fair down by some river side
I gaz-ed all around me an Irish girl I spied
So red and rosy were her cheeks and curly was her hair
And costly were those robes of gold this Irish girl did wear

Her shoes were of the Spanish black all sprinkled o'er with dew
She wrung her hands in terror saying Alas what shall I do?
I'm going home, I'm going home, I'm going home says she
What makes you go a roving and slight dear Pollee.

There's many a one so bad as he and why should I complain?
For love it is a killing thing did you ever feel the pain?
I wish my love was a red red rose and in some garden grew
With lilies I would garnish her, Sweet William, thyme and rue

THE IRISH GIRL

I wish I was a butterfly I would fly to my love's breast
I wish I was a linnet I would sing my love to rest
I wish I was a nightingale I'd sing till the morning clear
I would sit and sing to you Polly to the girl I love so dear

I wish I was in Manchester all seated on the grass
With a bottle of whisky in my hand and on my knee a lass
We'd call for liquors merrily and pay before we go
I'd roll her in my arms once more let the winds blow high or low.

[1310 Robert Parish at Exford 1907. Five other English and three American versions]
   2.2 She wrung her hands and tore her hair Good lord! what shall I do?
      [1908 Mr Edward Harrison at Langport 1909]
   2.3 *I'm going*: 1310 We're going. Most other versions have 'I'm'. 'Going home' is a common euphemism for 'dying'.

   3.1–3 These two lines, which occur in most versions, are supplied from
      1908.1908 has 'as bad as me', but other versions have 'he', which is obviously better sense.

   3.3–4 Another version has
    I wish my love was a red ripe rose that in the garden grows
    And I to be the gardener that's my love I would know

Other versions have minor variants, as 'coal black' for 'curly'; 'Exeter' for 'Manchester'; 'wine' for 'whisky'.

This song was widely popular; there are broadside versions and versions noted by collectors such as Lucy Broadwood (*English Traditional Songs and Carols*, 1908) and others (*Journal of the Folk-Song Society*, No. 1, 1899). There are numerous minor variations, but there is substantial agreement about the main elements of this somewhat confused narrative. This would suggest that all the versions have a common origin in the broadside issued by Such under the title *The New Irish Girl*. This title implies that there was an older *Irish Girl*, which may have been an earlier original. The author of this broadside may have combined elements from several songs without regard for logic. There appears to be an unexplained transition from one protagonist—the girl, to another—her lover.

No one, so far as I know, has reduced the narrative to order, and I have been unable to do so. The following points, however, are worth noting: the gold dress and shoes of Spanish leather imply a wealthy heroine (compare the heroine of *The Raggle-Taggle Gypsies*). I wonder if 'Irish' is a corruption of 'heiress'. The heroine is also connected with that of *The Foggy Dew* (No. 33). See 2.2 of *The Irish Girl*.

49 Jack Hall

My name it is Jack Hall chimney sweep, chimney sweep
My name it is Jack Hall chimney sweep.
My name it is Jack Hall and I'll rob both great and small
My neck shall pay for all when I die, when I die,
My neck shall pay for all when I die.

I've twenty cows in store that's no joke, that's no joke
I've twenty cows in store that's no joke
I've twenty cows in store and I'll rob for twenty more
My neck shall pay for all when I die when I die,
My neck shall pay for all when I die.

I've candles lily white that's no joke, that's no joke
I've candles lily white that's no joke
I've candles lily white O I stole them in the night
For to light me to the place where I lie, where I lie
For to light me to the place where I lie.

They tell me that in gaol I shall die I shall die
They tell me that in gaol I shall die
They tell me that in gaol I shall drink no more brown ale
But be dashed if ever I fail till I die, till I die
But be dashed if ever I fail till I die.

I rode up Tyburn's Hill in a cart in a cart
I rode up Tyburn's Hill in a cart
I rode up Tyburn's Hill and 'twas there I made my will
Saying the best of friends must part, so farewell, so farewell,
Saying the best of friends must part so farewell.

O I climbed up the ladder that's no joke that's no joke
O I climbed up the ladder that's no joke
O I climbed up the ladder and the hangman spread the rope
And the devil of a word said I coming down, coming down
And the devil of a word said I coming down

[82 Louie Hooper and Lucy White at Hambridge 1903
554 William Nott 1904]
    (No other version)

The above is a composite text using the whole of both versions.

JACK HALL

1.3 *and I'll rob both great and small*: 82 I have scandals great and small
1.4 *my neck*: 554 And my life
2.1 *cows*: evidently a sum of money. Partridge says the meaning '£1,000' dates from 1860; the song is much earlier, but this expression may have been introduced in the nineteenth century. In its context this meaning is preferable to loose woman, harlot', as signified by 'cow' in the eighteenth century.

Sharp published a slightly modified text in *Folk Songs from Somerset*, IV, 1908, and *English Folk Songs*, Selected Edition, 1921, Vol. II, with the following note: 'Jack Hall, who had been sold to a chimney sweep for a guinea, was executed for burglary at Tyburn in 1701.' He goes on to say that most of the tunes he collected were variants of the *Admiral Benbow* air. 'The metre in which each of these two ballads is cast is so unusual that we may assume that one was written in imitation of the other. As Jack Hall was executed in 1701 and Admiral Benbow was killed in 1702, *Jack Hall* is presumably the earlier of the two.'

A vulgarized version with a blasphemous chorus was current in the nineteenth century under the title of *Sam Hall*, and it is this which is recorded by Carl Sandburg.

50 *Joan's Ale was New*

There were seven jolly tradesmen
They all sat down together
They all sat down together
To make a jovial crew.
The first came in was a soldier
With his firelock on his shoulder
He throwed his firelock on the ground
Saying he'd wish every man would spend a crown
And let King Edward's health go round
When Joan's ale was new, my boys
When Joan's ale was new

JOAN'S ALE WAS NEW

The next come in was a mason
He had a sip out of the basin
He had a sip out of the basin
To make a jovial crew
He threw his hammer against the wall
Saying he wished every church and steeple may fall
Then it would be work for masons all
When Joan's ale was new, my boys
When Joan's ale was new

The next come in was a tailor
With bodkin shears and thimble
With bodkin shears and thimble
To make a jovial crew
He called for beer and then for chalk
Till this poor tailor was almost broke
And there he sat and pawned his coat
When Joan's ale was new, my boys
When Joan's ale was new

The next come in was a dyer
He sat himself down by the fire
He sat himself down by the fire
To make a jovial crew
He told the landlord plum to his face
The chimney corner was his place
And there he sat and dyed his face
When Joan's ale was new, my boys
When Joan's ale was new

The next come in was a hatter
To see what was the matter
To see what was the matter
To make a jovial crew
He throwed his hat all on the ground
Saying he'd wish every man would spend a crown
And swore King Edward's health should go round
When Joan's ale was new, my boys
When Joan's ale was new

JOAN'S ALE WAS NEW

The next come in was a tinker
He was no small beer drinker
He was no small beer drinker
To make a jovial crew
He mend but pots and then but kettles
His rivets were made of the best of metals
Good Lord how his hammer and pinchers did rattle
When Joan's ale was new, my boys
When Joan's ale was new

The next come in was a ragman
With his ragbag on his shoulder
With his ragbag on his shoulder
To make a jovial crew
He called for beer and then for glasses
Till they got drunk as any jackasses
And he burned the old ragbag all to ashes
When Joan's ale was new, my boys
When Joan's ale was new

[498 Jim Squires 1904. Three other versions]

1.9 *King Edward's*: 114 Victoria's. The name would be altered in accordance with the reigning sovereign.
1.10 *Joan's ale*: 498 Joan's saddle: but all other versions give 'Joan's ale'.
2.2 2068 He had a sip out of the basin: 498 With his hammer for a face'un.
2.6 *church and steeple*: 2176 and others: church and chapel
3.5 *chalk*: i.e. to mark up his debt.
4.7 *dyed his face*: cf. 'They call drinking deep, dyeing scarlet'. *Henry IV*, Part I, II. 4.

Sharp never printed this song, but versions of it are given by Durfey, Bell, Baring-Gould, Williams and others, proving that the song enjoyed currency over a long period. Bell (1857) says it was a lampoon on Oliver Cromwell, but his evidence is thin, and it is probable that it is considerably earlier. A 'ballet' of this name was entered in the stationers' register for 1594.

51 *Jolly Old Hawk*

(In this cumulative song, singers started either at the 'first day' and added one line at each repetition, or at the 'twelfth day' and omitted a line at each repetition and then built up again from two to twelve. Only the final repetition is here given, since it contains all the lines.)

A

Jolly old Hawk and his wings was grey
Now let us sing, who shall win the girl but me
Jolly old Hawk and his wings was grey
Send to my love the twelfthmost day
    Twelve old bears and they was roaring
    Eleven old mares and they was bawling
    Ten old cows as they was roaring
    Nine old whores and they was quarrelling
    Eight old bulls and they was a blaring
    Seven old calves as they cast afore them
    Six old cows as they was a roaring
    Five for fif and a fairy
    Four feeted pig
    Three fistle cock
    Two little birds and a jolly old ok

B

I went to my love the first to-day
It's a jolly old hawk and his wings was grey
Then let us see, then let us see
Who shall win this maid from me.

  2 It's a partridge bird, it's a partridge bird

  3 It's a three show cock, it's a three show cock

  4 It's a four-footed pig, it's a four-footed pig

  5 It's a five bears, it's a five bears

  6 It's a six hares, it's a six hares

JOLLY OLD HAWK

7 It's a seven cows had calved before

8 It's an eight churches stood before

9 It's a nine prisoners going a-shore

10 It's a ten cocks they were crowing

11 It's eleven carpenters they were yo-ing

12 It's a twelve sawyers they were sawing

[A 1243 William Chorley (72) at Bridgwater 1907
B Music Book 4934 Miss Priscilla Wyatt Sopell who had it from an old man 85 years old 1923]
(No other version)

A
line 12 fif and a fairy: inexplicable. It has been suggested that 'fieldfare' is intended.
13 *four* feeted *pig*: possibly four fitty pigs, i.e. fine or fittering (struggling): *Journal of the Folk-Song Society*, No. 20.
14 *fistle*: thristle, i.e. thrush.

B
14 *yo-ing*: hewing.

This song appears to have been published only in the *Journal of the Folk-Song Society*, No. 20, 1916, where Sharp printed the words of A unaltered. It is not the same song as *The Gay Goshawk* (Child) and its later variants. It is a cumulative song, like *The Twelve Days of Christmas*, to which it is distantly related, and seems to have been used in a game of forfeits during Christmas celebrations. Its origin may be French; one of the tunes is similar to that of *Gently Johnny my Jingalo* (No. 34). Both bear some resemblance to the tune of Auprès *de ma blonde*, whose theme also is distantly related. These tunes are similar to that of *London Bridge is Broken Down*, which was a children's dance game known in medieval France and elsewhere (see Opie, *Oxford Dictionary of Nursery Rhymes*).

The goshawk is a symbol for an inconstant mistress. The theme is that of winning her favour by a series of gifts, as in *The Twelve Days of Christmas*. The gifts here are grotesque in character.

52 *The Keeper*

O the keeper he a shooting goes
And all amongst his bucks and does
And O for to shoot at the barren doe
She's amongst the leaves of the green O.
    Jacky boy. Martin
        Sing 'ee well. Very well
        Hey Down Ho down
        Derry derry down

She's amongst the leaves of the green O.
To my hey down down
To my ho down down
Hey down, ho down
Derry derry down
She's amongst the leaves of the green O.

The first doe that he shot at he missed
And the second doe he trimmed he kissed
And the third ran away in a young man's heart
She's amongst the leaves of the green O.

The fourth doe then she crossed the plain
The keeper fetched her back again
O and he tickled her in a merry vein
She's amongst the leaves of the green O.

The fifth doe then she crossed the brook
The keeper fetched her back with his long hook
And what he done at her you must go and look
For she's amongst the leaves of the green O.

[2112 Robert Kinchin (63) at Ilmington 1909. Two other versions]

  1.3 *barren*: unmated.
  2.2 *trimmed*: stripped.

THE KEEPER

> The whole of this stanza is replaced in 920 by
>> The very first Doe that tripped over the hill
>> The keeper helped himself on the hill
>> A watching of his Does.
>> Master Chalker can you sing
>> Very well lie down low down
>> Deny derry down, deny deny down
>> And amongst the leaves so green oh.

3.3. *merry*: lascivious.

The theme of sexual pursuit symbolized by a hunt is a commonplace in medieval poetry. A severely neutralized version of this song was published by Sharp in Novello's *School Songs* (1909) and again in *English Folk Songs*, Selected Edition, 1921, Vol. II. The only other editor to have published the song is Baring-Gould (*Songs of the West*, 1890), who wrote: 'I have been compelled to rewrite most of the song, which in the original is very gross. It is certainly an ancient composition.'

In the refrain, published texts give 'Master' for 'Martin'. This refrain is in dialogue form and suggests some activity such as drinking or hawking, but I am not sure what. 'Derry down' is described in the *Shorter Oxford English Dictionary* as 'a meaningless refrain', but it seems to be connected with the obscene sexual dance mentioned by Dunbar in *Ane Brash of Wowing*:

> Syne tha twa till ane play began,
> Quhilk that thay call the dirrydan.

In *The Twa Corbies* this refrain appears to be a lament, but possibly the ballad was no more than tragi-comic.

53 *The Kettle Smock*

> A-shailing and toiling as I was one day
> The thought of my love it led me astray
> The day it was gone and the night coming on
> And I ran away with my kettle smock on
>
> When to my love's window crying are you in bed?
> No sooner she heard me she lifted her head.
> She lifted her head and cried Is that John?
> Yes indeed it is me with my kettle smock on.
>
> She opened the door and invited me in
> Draw up to the fire and warm up your shin
> The bedroom door opened and blankets turned down
> And I rolled into bed with my kettle smock on.

THE KETTLE SMOCK

We tumbled and tasted till the break of day
Forgetting the hours that we passed away
Till my love she jumped up and cried what have you done
The baby will come with a kettle smock on.

I chastised my love for speaking so wild
You stupid young girl you'll ne'er have a child
For all that I've done I reckon but fun
And I ran away with my kettle smock on

So come all you young maidens where'er you may be
Remember the chaps that are single and free
For their hearts d'run light and their minds d'run young
So beware of the chaps with the kettle smocks on.

[1166 William Stokes at Chew Stoke 1907. No other version]

Kettle smock: Sharp's ms. says this means 'cattle smock', but for another sense of 'kettle' see note on *The Brisk Young Bachelor* (No. 19). This is confirmed by the close similarity of the song to a Scottish version noted by Mr Patrick Shuldham-Shaw in the Shetlands, of which the refrain is 'Wi' my coortin' coat on'.

54 *Keys of Heaven*

A

Madam I'll present to you a fine silken gown
With four and twenty yards for to draggle on the ground
If you'll be my joy and on-er-ly sweet dear
And walk along with me anywhere.

Madam I'll present to you a fine silver ball
To tumble in your garden the finest day of all
If you'll be . . .

Madam I'll present to you a fine silver chest
With a key of gold and silver and jewels of the best
If you'll be . . .

KEYS OF HEAVEN

Madam I'll present to you a set of new bells
To call up your servants when you are not well
If you'll be . . .

O Madam I will give to you the Keys of Canterbury
And all the bells of London will ring and make us merry
If you'll be my joy and on-er-ly sweet dear
And walk along with me anywhere.

B

O my man John what can the matter be
You see I love the lady and she won't love me
She won't be my bride my joy nor my dear
She won't go walking with me anywhere

You court her, court her master, you court her never fear
There's a time she'll walk and be your only dear
There's a time she'll walk and be your only dear
And go walking with you anywhere

O Madam I will give to thee a new silk gown
With five and thirty flounces a bobbing to the ground
If you will be my bride my joy and my dear
If you'll go a walking with me anywhere

O I won't accept of your new silk gown
With five and thirty flounces a bobbing to the ground
Nor I won't be your bride your joy and your dear
Nor I won't go a walking with you anywhere

O Madam I'll present you with boots made of cork
One was made in London and one was made in York
If you will be . . .

O I won't accept of your boots made of cork
One was made in London and one was made in York
Nor I won't be . . .

KEYS OF HEAVEN

O Madam I will give to you your apron full of gold
And twice as much more as your apron it will hold
If you will be . . .

O I won't accept of your apron full of gold
Nor twice as much more as my apron it will hold
Nor I won't be . . .

O Madam I will give you a bed of down so soft
For you to lay under and I to lay aloft
If you will be . . .

O I won't accept of your bed of down so soft
For me to lay under and you to lay aloft
Nor I won't be . . .

O Madam I'll present you with a little golden bell
To ring up your servants when you are not well
If you will be . . .

O I won't accept of your little golden bell
To ring up my servants when I am not well
Nor I won't be . . .

O Madam I will give to you a fine gold pin
To pin up your baby clothes when you do lay in
If you will be . . .

O I won't accept of your fine gold pin
To pin up my baby clothes when I do lay in
Nor I won't be . . .

O Madam I'll present to you the key of my heart
The day that we get married we'll never more depart
If you will be . . .

Indeed I will accept of you the key of your heart
I'll lock it up for ever and never more to part
And I will be your bride your joy and your dear
And I'll go a walking with you anywhere

KEYS OF HEAVEN

O my man John here's fifty pound for you
For all you've told me it is come true
She will be my bride my joy and my dear
She will go walking with me anywhere.

[A 537 Mrs Welch senior at He Bruers 1904
809 Mrs Harriet Young at West Chirmach 1905]
[B 531 Mrs Glover 1904
1367 Mrs Beer (78) at Killerton 1908
1696 Mrs Gulliford at Combe Florey 1908
926 Susan Williams at Haselbury 1906]

Sharp noted twelve versions of *The Keys of Heaven* and *My Man John*, which are the same song, though the former does not introduce the serving-man, who is variously called 'My man John', 'my man Jan' and 'old man Jan'. It is usually in dialogue form, the man offering and the woman refusing gifts in alternate stanzas. Three of Sharp's ms. versions give only the lover's stanzas, as in A. The song was noted by other collectors; all versions are essentially the same, the only material differences being in the gifts offered—apart from those enumerated in A and B, other versions mentioned: a fine coach and pair, a coach and six, house and land, rings and jewels, a world of treasure, a little grey-hound, an ivory comb, a cushion full of pins, a blue silk gown, a fine beaver hat, and a fine knit cap.

Baring-Gould's version (*Songs of the West*, 1890) is entitled *Blue Muslin*, which is the first of the offerings. The lover also offers shoes of cork. According to Baring-Gould, muslin was introduced into England in 1670, and cork in 1690.

The tone of the song varies in different versions between the romantic, the materialistic, and the realistic. In view of the variety of the versions in Sharp's ms., and of their equal merit, I have given two composite texts, one in a romantic, the other in a realistic strain. I have felt justified in introducing stanza 4 of A from another version than those listed, and in transferring stanzas 9 and 10 of B from 809, since none of the ms. versions is entirely congruous and all enumerate a varied selection of offerings. While some of these offerings are purely material, others—such as the silver ball and the apron full of gold —are to be interpreted on the plane of sexual symbolism.

None of Sharp's versions is wholly materialistic in tone. He published a romantic and somewhat modified version in *Folk Songs from Somerset*, III, 1906, and in *English Folk Songs*, Selected Edition, 1921, Vol. II, and two other versions in the *Journal of the Folk-Song Society*, No. 7, 1915.

I have retained the title used for the majority of Sharp's ms. versions, even though 'Heaven' is never mentioned.

The song is closely related to O *No John*, No. 68.

55 *Lancashire Lass*

Here's to the maid in Lancashire Town
Here's to the maid in the cadelico
I vow and declare he loved her so dear
'Cause she did wear pretty caps upon her hair
        Fol the dol the day

Says Master unto Missus I'm going out of town
Says Missus unto Betsy, You go unto your bed
And I for your Master
Will wait up in your stead.

Twelve o'clock came and knock was at the door
Missus went out to see who was there
And on the cold ground he tumbled her down
And into her hand he put half a crown

Horses out in stable a making of a noise
Master went out to see who was there
Missus croped upstairs and laughed at the fun
To think how the maid and the master was undone

Next morning at breakfast the bell she did ring
Saying here's half a crown that your master gave to me
And many a bright crown has he turned unto thee

She tooked her by the shoulders and led her to the door
Saying There's no home for a wife and a wench
For all this long time I never can endure
For I can't come in for a morsel of my share

And all that they done, they done in a month
And after that they turned bump to bump.
        Fol the dol day

[469 Mrs Overd's words 1904. No other version]
1.2 *cadelico*: dialect form of calico
5.1 *she*: 469 he
I have discovered no text of this song, so that the obviously defective lines cannot be supplied. *The Frolicsome Farmer*, a broadside reprinted in *The Common Muse* (V. de Sola Pinto and A. E. Rodway, Chatto & Windus, 1957), relates the same story in a fuller and rather more refined form.

56 *The Lark in the Morn*

As I was a-walking one morning in the Spring
I met a young damsel so sweetly she did sing
And as we were a walking these words she did say
No life like a ploughboy in the month of May.

The lark in the morn she rise from her nest
She mounts in the air with the dew on her breast
And with her sweet ploughboy she'll whistle and sing
At midnight return to her nest back again.

Here's Allie, here's Dolly, here's Kate and here's Sue.
And here's Jack, Will and Tom and old Johnny too
Come lads take yer lasses and away to the Fair
So do they lark relish, I vow and declare

So as they were walking from the Wick to the Town
Where the meadows are mown and the grass is cut down
And if one should stumble amongst this green hay
Kiss me now or never this damsel did say

'Twas down in that meadow in that private Park
Where he kissed me sweetly and he gained my heart
Where his kisses so sweet and his humour so free
In spite of my own heart which made me agree.

What will a young woman do with an old man
She'll bring him a cuckold as soon as she can
She'll roast him in onions and pound him in 'ot
Rub salt in his eyes and they'll rock him asleep

[720 John Dingle at Coryton 1905. No other version]

1.1-2 These lines are not in 720. They have been supplied from printed texts in which several editors agree, Sharp included.

6.3-4 Evidently a way of roasting a cuckoo, symbolizing the cuckolding of an old man. These two lines are followed in the ms. by And her oles mine!

Sharp published the first two stanzas, more or less as printed above, in *Folk Songs from Somerset*, V, 1909, in Novello's *School Songs*, 1909, and again in

English Folk Songs, Selected Edition, 1921, Vol. II. In a note he says: 'As, however, the extra verses seem to me to detract from rather than to add to the beauty of the song, I have thought it better to dispense with them.' Kidson and other editors also give abridged texts, and refer to more complete broadside texts. One of these is entitled *The Plowman's Glory*. Editors in the past have been at pains to stress the lyrical at the expense of the social implications of this song. We need no longer feel obliged to ignore the sexual significance of 'lark' in the colloquial sense, nor other obvious sexual references throughout the song.

According to a quotation in Sharp's *Life* (1955 edition, p. 39), this song was collected in memorable circumstances. 'Cecil Sharp had heard that a song which he had not hitherto recorded was known in an out-of-the-way corner of England.' An old woman who knew it was working in her garden. She grasped the lapels of his coat, closed her eyes, and sang in a 'quavering yet beautiful voice', while Sharp made rapid notes. 'When the song was finished, she gazed into his eyes in a sort of ecstasy, and, in perfect detachment from herself exclaimed, "Isn't it lovely!"' Sharp's notebooks, however, contain no version of *The Lark in the Morn* taken down from a woman, the only one being the above.

57 *The London, Man of War*

On the 21st of August in Plymouth Sound we lay
Our orders come on board my boys we could no longer stay
'Twas on the coast of Ireland, our orders did run so
All for to cruise and never refuse to meet with our proud foe.

We had not sailed many a league before we chanced to spy
A long and lofty man o 'war come bearing down on us so nigh
He hailed us in French my boys from where and whence we came
Our answer was 'from Liverpool Bright London is our name.'

If you're the London man o' war as I suppose you be
We are the royal Delamore and that you soon shall see
So I pray haul up your courses and let your ship lay to
Your mainsail stow it and boats hoist out or else we will sink you.

THE LONDON, MAN OF WAR

The first broadside we give to them, it struck them with such a wonder
To see their yards and topmasts too come rattling down like thunder
That's very well, that's very well our Captain he did say
That's very well said the Commodore, we'll show them British play

The next broadside we give to them so hot our shots did fly
We shot away their Ensign staff and down their colours lay
That's very well, that's very well, our Captain he did say
Your swords now draw, your pistols load, we'll board without delay

Now we have taken the Delamore safe into Plymouth Sound
And when she has come to an anchor boys we'll fire our guns all round
So here's a health to our Captain and all such warlike souls
To him we'll drink and never flinch, Round with the flowing bowl.

[387 Captain Lewis 1904. One other version]

This was printed after Sharp's death in the *Journal of the Folk-Song Society*, No. 31, 1927, but I have not seen it elsewhere, and I have been unable to discover anything about the action described.

58 *Long and Wishing Eye*

As Johnny walked out one fine summer's morn
And there he hid himself all under a thorn
And there he spied a fair pretty maid as she was passing by
Young Johnny followed after, with a long and wishing eye

Have you seen my ewe with its two little lambs
Strayed away from their home, strayed away from their dams.
O yes, O yes, fair pretty maid, I saw them two pass by
I was down in yonder valley love, and that is very nigh.

O she traced the valley over; no lambs could she find
And often times she cursed this young man in her mind
She turned herself most curiously, and followed and smiled with a blush
While Johnny followed after was hidden in the bush.

O the patience of love it began to overflow
And Johnny he tookèd her in the valley down below
When he hugged her, he kissed her, his joys to renew
Where the lambs skipped all round them, all in the morning dew.

And now to conclude and to finish my song
I left a happy couple in the heats of their fun
So now they are got married, they're joined in wedlock bands
No more I'll go a roving in searching of young lambs

[137 William Nott at Meshaw 1904. Two other versions]

    1.4   *long and wishing*: a corruption of languishing
    4.4   1233 No more they go a courting all in the morning dew
    5.4   137 repeats this line as a Chorus:
    In searching of young lambs my boy
    I'll go no more a-roving
    In searching of young lambs.

59 Lord Thomas of Winesberry

As I looked over high Castle wall
For to see what I could see
And who should I saw but my own father's ship
Which come sailing home from sea, from sea, from sea
Which come sailing home from sea.

What's the matter my daughter Jane
What do make you look so worn
For I'm afraid you've had some ill sickness
Or been sleeping with some young man, young man,
    young man
Or been sleeping with some young man.

I've not had no ill sickness
Nor sleeping with no young man
But I have been so sick to the heart
Since you've been so long from home

Then off she took her gown of green
And throwed it on the ground
Her underclothing it was so short
She was full three quarters gone.

Is it by a noble knight
Or a lord of high degrees
Or is it by that dirty sailor boy
That sails along with me?

O it's neither by a noble knight
Or a lord of high degrees
It is by that Jolly Jack Tar
That sails along with thee.

Will you marry my daughter Jane
And marry her out of hand
And prove a father to the child
I'll share you out my land

LORD THOMAS OF WINESBERRY

I will marry your daughter Jane
I will marry her out of hand
And prove a father to her child
But I values not your land.

[952   John Barnett at Bridgwater 1906. Two other versions]

  2.2   *worn*: probably 'wan'
  6.3   *It is*: 952 Is it

811   (Mr Gordge of Bridgwater 1906) gives for stanza 4
  O she pulled off her gown of green
  And she hanged it against the wall
  Her stays would not meet nor her approm strings tie
  O she's full three quarters gone

Sharp gives a text of this ballad in *Folk Songs from Somerset*, v, 1909, and *English Folk Songs*, Selected Edition, 1921, Vol. I, in which he omits stanza 4 and makes other modifications. He retains the title used by Child, who prints several versions. The story varies in detail from version to version. The text given above omits one essential step: in one of Child's texts the girl's father disbelieves her and orders her to cast off her gown.

In another version collected by Sharp (*The Laird of Whinesbarren*) an Irishman's daughter is questioned by her father about her pregnancy, and replies that the lover was not a noble lord, a gentleman or 'that rakish lad that is now returned from Spain', but one of her father's servants, William. The father invites William to sup and dine with him and to be his heir; he accepts the former invitation but contemptuously declines his land on the ground that he has land and wealth himself, and only entered the lord's service on account of his daughter. Elsewhere the lover is variously named Johnny Barbary, Tom the Barber and Willie o' Winsbury.

60 *The Lowlands of Holland*

The very first day I got married
That night I lay on my bed
A Press gang came to my bedside
These words to me did say
Saying Arise Arise young man they said
And go along with me
To the low low lands of Holland
To face your enemy.

But Holland is a cold place
A place where grows no green
But Holland is a cold place
For my love to wander in
But money had been so plentiful
As leaves grow on the tree
And before I'd time to turn myself
My love was stolen from me.

I'll build my love a ship
A ship of noted fame
I'd have four and twenty seamen bold
To box her on the main.
They will rant and roar in sparkling glee
Where some ever they do go
To the low low lands of Holland
To face the daring foe

Says the mother to the daughter
What makes you to lament
Neither lords nor dukes nor squires
Can give my heart content
Nor neither will I married be
Until the day I die
Since the low low lands of Holland
Have parted my love and I.

THE LOWLANDS OF HOLLAND

There's not a swish goes round my waist
Nor a comb goes in my hair
Neither fire light nor candle light
Can ease my heart's despair
Nor neither will I married be
Until the day I die
Since the low low lands of Holland
Have parted my love and I.

[630 Robert Dibble at Bridgwater 1905. Two other English versions and a fragment; one American fragment]

2.2 *grows*: 630 goes
2.5 *But money*, etc. Version defective, but the meaning appears to be: If I had had money, I could have bought him off. As it was, he was taken away before I had time to turn round.
3.4 *box*: hurry.
3.6 *Where some ever*: wheresoever.
4.3 *Neither*: 630 May the
4.4 *give my heart*: 630 ease my heart's
5.1 *swish*: 280 swaise. Dialect or archaic words for sash.

Sharp published this text, almost without alteration, in *Folk Songs from Somerset*, II, 1905, and *English Folk Songs*, Selected Edition,1921, Vol. II. Interesting variants in his other versions are: for 1.7-8 'To the Lowlands Low in Amerikee And fight your enemy' (280 Benjamin Horler at East Hampton 1904); 872 (Walter Locock at Martock 1906) has

    Crying the old man to his daughter
    What make you so lament
    For there's many a lad in our town
    Can give your heart content
    There's many a lad in our town
    But there's not one for me
    The rough seas and the storm and wind
    Parted my true love and me
    No lace shan't go round my waist
    No comb shan't go through my hair
    No handkerchief shan't go round my neck
    To hide my bosom fair.

For 'our town' a fragmentary version (363) has 'Gallant Town', which I take to be 'Galway'. Mr Philander Fitzgerald of Nashville, Nelson County, Virginia (1918) had

    O Holland is a pretty place
    All strewed with the lasses round.

The song was published in various versions from the eighteenth century onwards, some of them Scottish and Irish.

61 *Maid Freed from the Gallows*

O the prickly briar
It pricks my heart so sore
If I once get out of the prickly bush
I'll never get in no more

O hangman hold your hand
And hold it for a while
For I think I see my father coming
Across the yonder stile.
   O the prickly briar . . .

Oh! have you got my gold
And can you set me free
Or are you come to see me hung
Upon the gallows-tree
   O the prickly briar . . .

Oh! I've not got your gold
Nor I can't set you free
But I have come to see you hung
Upon the gallows tree
   O the prickly briar . . .

The song continues with 'mother', 'brother' *and* 'sister', *ending with*:

O hangman hold your hand
And hold it for a while
For I think I see my true love coming
Across the yonder stile
   O the prickly briar . . .

Oh! have you got my gold
And can you set me free
Or are you come to see me hung
Upon the gallows tree
   O the prickly briar . . .

MAID FREED FROM THE GALLOWS

Oh yes I've got your gold
And I can set you free
For I'm not come to see you hung
Upon the gallows tree.
   O the prickly briar
   It pricks my heart so sore
   Now I'm once got out of the prickly bush
   I'll never get in no more

[1883 noted in Langport by Miss Bertha Paul and sent to Sharp by the Rev. D. M. Ross 1908. One other English and eight American versions]
2.3 *I think*: 1902 I fancy (throughout)
Final refrain 4th line: *no more*: 1883 it again
248 Mr T. Jeff. Stockton at Hogskin Creek, Flag Pond, Ten.1916:
Hold up your hand and Joshua she cries
And wait a little while and see.
I think I hear my father dear
Come lumbering here for to see.

O father O father have you any gold for me
Or silver to pay my fee.
They say I've stoled a silver cup
And hanged I must be.

No 'prickly briar' refrain. Another American version has 'golden cup' instead of 'silver', as above. Another American version has 'Beneath the willow tree' instead of 'Upon the gallows-tree'.

Sharp prints this song, substantially as above, under the title *The Briery Bush* in *Folk Songs from Somerset*, 1909, and *English Folk Songs*, Selected Edition, 1921, Vol. II. Other editors print similar versions. I have retained the title used by Child, and in Sharp's ms. The texts printed by Child have no refrain, but are generally longer than the folk song versions. In a Scottish version given by Child, the girl, after being rescued by her lover, curses each of her relatives in turn with force and pungency. In these ballad versions 'Lord Judge' is usually given instead of 'Hangman', and in the American version quoted above 'Judge' becomes 'Joshua'.

   Child relates the ballad to numerous versions found all over the Continent, in which the girl has been captured by pirates, who hold her up to ransom. He appears to consider the English versions inferior because they give no reason for the girl's predicament, but he was unaware of the allegorical significance of the story as proved by the discovery of its connection with the legend of 'The Golden Ball' (Joseph Jacobs, *More English Fairy Tales*).
   In this story, a girl receives a golden ball from a mysterious stranger; if she loses it she will be hung. While she is playing with it, it is spirited away from

her, and she is condemned to death. She vainly appeals to her relations to recover it for her; in the end her lover recovers it just in time to save her, and they are married. The story was also acted as folk drama in England at least until the late nineteenth century.

This information is taken from an account given in the *Journal of the Folk-Song Society*, No. 19, 1915, by A. G. Gilchrist, who points out that gold was regarded as a symbol of integrity; the girl had lost her honour through a disastrous seduction, possibly by a supernatural lover. Her honour and her happiness could be restored only by the courage and forgiveness of her true lover.

The 'prickly bush' has a dual significance. It represents a fatal love-entanglement, as in *Waly Waly* (No. 108), and it recalls the more primitive legendary punishment for incontinence, burning.

62 Man of War

I married a wife and her name was Grace.
I oftimes cursed her ugly face,
Saying: It's you that has brought me to this disgrace
On board of the man of war O.

They hung me up by my two thumbs,
And they cut me till the blood did run,
And that was the usage that they gave me
On board of the man of war O.

If I could get my one foot on shore
Some other pretty girl I'd marry once more;
Neither the winds nor the waves should entice me any more
On board of the man of war O.

[3348 Mr Taylor at Ross Workhouse 1921. No other version]

63 The Miller and the Lass

A brisk young lass so brisk and gay
She went unto the mill one day
There's a peck of corn all for to grind
The devil of the miller could she find

But alas the miller he did come in
And this fair maid she did begin
There's a peck of corn all for to grind
I can but stay a little time

Come sit you down my sweet pretty dear
I cannot grind your corn I fear
My stones is high and my water low
I cannot grind for the mill won't go

Then she sat down all on a sack
They talked of this and they talked of that
They talked of love, of love proved kind
She soon found out the mill would grind

Then he got up the mill to grind
And left her down the stones to mind
Then an easy up and down
She scarce could tell when her corn was ground

Then go you home my sweet pretty dear
The corn is ground and the mill is clear
She swore she'd been ground by a score or more
But never been ground so well before.

[1060 William Bailey (60) at Connington 1906. One other fragmentary version]
    2.4 *can but*: 1060 cannot

The association of millers with ribaldry goes back at least as far as Chaucer's *Revels Tale* and its French and Italian sources. Partridge traces this meaning of 'stones' to the twelfth century, and of 'grind' to the late sixteenth century.

64 *Mowing the Barley*

A Lawyer he went out one day,
A for to take his pleasure,
And who should he spy but some fair pretty girl
So handsome and so clever.
>   Where are you going to my pretty maid?
>   Where are you going my honey?
>   I'm over the hills kind sir she said
>   To my father a mowing the barley

The Lawyer he went out next day
A -thinking for to view her;
But she gave him the slip and away she went
All over the hills to her father.
>   Where are you going to . . .

This lawyer had a useful nag,
And soon he overtook her.
He caught her by the waist so small
And on his horse he placed her
>   Saying hold up your cheeks, my fair pretty maid
>   Hold up your cheeks my honey
>   That I may give you a fair pretty kiss
>   And a handful of gold and silver

Oh keep your gold and silver too
And take it where you're going;
For there's many a rogue and scamp like you
Has brought poor girls to ruin

But now she is the Lawyer's wife
And the Lawyer loves her dearly
They live in the happiest content of life
And will in the place above here

[131 William Spearing at He Bruers 1904. No other version]

Sharp printed this song substantially as given here in *Folk Songs from Somerset*, I, 1904, and *English Folk Songs*, Selected Edition, 1921, Vol. I, but inserted after stanza 4 another stanza, from what source he does not say, concerning the lawyer's courtship. Otherwise his principal emendation is of the final line, which his texts give as 'And well in the station above her'.

65 My Bonny Bonny Boy

O once I was courted by a bonny bonny boy
I loved him I vow and protest
I loved him so well and so very well
That I built him a bower in my breast

It's up the green meadows and down the steep valleys
Like one that was troubled in mind
I hollooed and hooped and played on my flute
But no bonny bonny boy could I find

I set myself down on the green mossy bank
Where the sun it shone wonderful warm
And who did I spy but my own bonny boy
Fast locked in some other girl's arms

Some say my bonny boy has gone over the main
God send him good luck to return
But if he loves another girl better than me
Let him love her and why should I mourn.

Now the girl that does enjoy my bonny bonny boy
I'm sure she is never to blame
For many a long night he has robbed me of my rest
But he never shall do it again.

[1482 Mrs Elizabeth Smitherd at Tewkesbury 1908
1356 Miss Sarah Smith at Gray's Inn Road (no date)]
 (No other version)
1.4 *That I built him a bower in my breast* 1356: 1482 has That I could build
 him a nest in my heart
 5 1356 (not in 1482)

Sharp gives a text in *English Folk Songs*, Selected Edition, 1921, Vol. I, which omits stanza 4, and replaces 'he' by 'she' in 5.3-4. Versions were popular from the time of Charles II. Kidson said (*Journal of the Folk-Song Society*, No. 7, 1905): 'The various versions collected all point to one original, I believe, and that is undoubtedly very old.' There is good reason to think that this original would give 'bird' for 'boy'. 'Bird' occurs in some seventeenth- and eighteenth-century broadside texts. This gives point to expressions like 'a nest in my heart' and 'I hollooed and hooped'. Baring-Gould (*Songs of the West*, 1890) goes so far as to state categorically that the song is a counterpart of *The Gay Goshawk*.

66 *My Valentine*

'Twas Valentine's day come early in the morn
Come early in the morn betime
A fair young damsel came at my bedside
And she would fain be my Valentine

'Twas two or three months came on after this
This young woman came riding by
She said Kind Sir I'm with child by thee
And the same thing you never can't deny.

If you are by child my fair pretty one
The child is not none of mine
Unless that you can tell me how where and when
The very same hour and time.

It is I that can tell you how where and when
The very same hour and time
And if you don't consent to marry me
In some prison I'll have you close confined

Then he gave consent the very next morn
To be married without any more delay
But instead of being married to this poor girl
He took shipping and soon sailed away.

He's gone he's gone the Lord he don't know where
Perhaps his body may be floating in the sea
But if ever he live to return back again
I will thank him for his kindness unto me

Seven long years been absent past and gone
This young man came rolling home in gold
So she never once rebuked him for his long abstent
But she couraged him for being so bold.

MY VALENTINE

[395 Mrs Overd 1904
738 James Bishop at Hunter's Lodge Priddy 1905]
   (One other fragment)

   6 This stanza is taken from 738. It is very similar in 395, but lacks half of line 3.

The only other published text of this song is an edited one by Kidson (*Folk Songs from the North Countrie*, 1927). In *Traditional Tunes*, 1891, he had excused himself from printing more than the first stanza on the ground that 'the whole song is poor doggrel'.

Like Ophelia's song (*Hamlet*, IV. 5) it is based on the ancient custom by which a man was supposed to marry the first girl he saw on St Valentine's Day.

67 *O Dear O*

As I was walking one midsummer morning
To view the fields and the leaves a springing
There was two birds upon the tree
Sounding their notes and sweetly singing
   O dear O what shall I do?
My husband got no courage in him
                              O dear O!

All sorts of meat I did provide
All sorts of drink that are fitting for him
But oyster pie and rhubarb too
But nothing would put courage in him
   O dear O what shall I do
My husband got no courage in him
                              O dear O!

My husband's admired wherever he go
And every one looked well upon him
By his hands and feet and well shaped eye
But still he got no courage in him
   O dear O what shall I do
My husband got no courage in him
                              O dear O!

O DEAR O

Seven long years I made his bed
Six of them I lay beside him
And this morning I rose with my maidenhead
For still he had no courage in him
    O dear O what shall I do
My husband got no courage in him
                              O dear O!

I wish the Lord that he were dead
And in his grave I quickly lay him
Then I'd try another one
That had a little courage in him
    O dear O what shall I do
My husband got no courage in him
                              O dear O!

[483 George Wyatt 1904. Two other versions]

1.6   *in him*: 483 in his
2.3   oysters are a notorious aphrodisiac, but rhubarb is less well known in this connection.
3.1   *husband's*: 483 husband
3.3   *By his hands and feet*: 483 But his hands once feet. This line is obviously corrupt. I have made what sense I can of it with the minimum of alteration.

Another version (1094 John Vincent, 72, at Hampton Lodge, Priddy 1906) has for 1.3–7

I saw two maidens standing by
And one of them her hands was wringing
And all of her conversation were
My husband got no courage in him.

It has also an additional stanza:

Come all pretty maidens wherever you be
Don't love a man before you try him
Lest you should sing a song with me
My husband's got no courage in him

68 O No John

On yonder hill there stands a creature
Who she is I do not know
I'll go and court her for her beauty
She must answer Yes or No
   O No John, No John, No John No.

On her bosom are bunches of posies
On her breast where flowers grow
If I should chance to touch that posy
She must answer Yes or No
   O No John, No John, No John No.

Madam I am come for to court you
Whether your passions I can gain
Come and set yourself down alongside of me
Fear I should never see you again
   O No John, No John, No John No.

My husband he was a Spanish Captain
Went to sea but a month ago
And the very last time we kissed and parted
He always bid me answer No.
   O No John, No John, No John No.

Madam in your face is beauty
In your bosom flowers grow
In your bedroom there is pleasure
Shall I view it, yes or no?
   O No John, No John, No John No.

Madam shall I tie your garter
Tie it a little above your knee
If my hand should slip a little farther
Would you think it amiss of me?
   O No John, No John, No John No.

My love and I we went to bed together
There we lay till the cocks did crow
Unclose your arms my dearest jewel
Unclose your arms and let me go
   O No John, No John, No John No.

O NO JOHN

[1285 William Morley at Bincombe 1907
1777 James Beale (72) at Wareham, Kent 1908
81   Lucy White and Louie Hooper at Hambridge 1903
1457 Alfred Emery (78) at Othery 1908]
   (No other English versions, three American)

As none of these versions contains the whole story, I have given a composite text using the four versions enumerated above.

   5.2 *In your bosom flowers grow*: 81 In you flowers grow

(For a full discussion of this song, see Introduction, pp. 33–37).

69 *Ripest Apples*

   Yonder sits a Spanish lady
   Who she is I do not know
   I'll go and court her for her beauty
   Whether she answers Yes or No

   Madam I am come a courting
   If your favour I can gain
   If you will entertain me
   Perhaps then I might come again

   Madam I have rings and jewels
   Madam I have houses and lands
   Madam I have the world of treasure
   And all shall be at your command

   What cares I for rings and jewels
   What cares I for houses and lands
   What cares I for the world of treasure
   So as I have a handsome man.

   Madam you think much of beauty
   Beauty's a flower soon does fade
   The finest flower in your garden
   Will soon fade and die away

Ripest apples soon does a rotten
Young woman's beauty soon does agay
You pick a flower all in the morning
Until at night it withers away

So I tooked her up in that very fine chamber
And there we laid all on the bed
And there we laid all cuddled together
And the very next morning I made her my bride.

First comes night and then comes day
So we pass our time away
First come young ones then come old ones
So we pass our time away

[2015 William Shepherd (93) at Winchcombe 1909
1125 William Davis at Porlock Weir 1906]
 (No other English versions, three American)
2015 is given in ms. under the title *O No John*. Stanzas 1, 2, 3, 4, 5 and 8 are from this. Remaining stanzas from 1125.
   6.2 agay: decay.
(For discussion of this song, see Introduction, pp. 33–37.)

70 *On Monday Morning I Married a Wife*

On Monday morning I married a wife
Thinking to live a sober life
I wish to God she had been dead
Before I'd enjoyed her maidenhead
  Laddy-i-o laddy-i-o
  Fol de rol lol de rol, Laddy-i-o.

On Tuesday morning I went to the' ood
Thinking to do my wife some good
I cut her a twig of the holly so green
The finest of twigs as ever was seen.

On Wednesday morning I hung it out to dry
On Thursday morning I did it try
I beat her all over the shoulders and head
Till I had a broke my holly green twig.

ON MONDAY MORNING I MARRIED A WIFE

On Friday morning at my surprise
A little before the sun did rise
She opened her mouth and began to roar
I thought to myself that she'd never give o'er.

On Saturday morning I breakfast without
A scolding wife or a brawling bout
Now I can enjoy my bottle and friend
I think I had made a rare week i'end

[1164   Mrs R. Sage at Chew Stoke 1907. One other version]
  1.4   *maidenhead*: 1164 maiden head
  1.5–6   *Laddy-i-o*: 1164 Laddy I. O.
  2.1   *'ood*: dialect form of wood.
  2.3   *holly*: the symbol of male domination.

Baring-Gould (*Songs of the West*, 1890) gives an edited version, and says that the song was common as a broadside and in eighteenth-century song-collections. Here several preliminary stanzas were usually given describing the bachelor's gay life before marriage. Baring-Gould's version has the following interesting stanza, of which unfortunately he does not state the source:

On Saturday morn, as I may say,
As she on her pillow consulting [? insulting—J. R.] lay
A Bogie arrived in fume and flame,
And carried her off both blind and lame.

71 *Our Captain Cried All Hands*

Our captain cried all hands
And away tomorrow
Leaving these girls behind
In grief and sorrow.

What makes you go abroad
Fighting for strangers
When you could stop at home
Free from all dangers.

OUR CAPTAIN CRIED ALL HANDS

You courted me a while
Just to deceive me
Now my heart you have gained
You means to leave me

Saying there's no belief in man
Not my own brother
So girls if you can love
Love one another

When I had the gold in store
You did invite me
Now I'm low and poor
You seems to slight me.

Dry off your brandy tears
And leave off weeping
For happy shall we be
At our next meeting.

[334 Mrs Overd 1904. One other version]

3.2 *can*: 1483 must
6.1 *brandy*: 1483 mountain. Just as the latter is obviously a corruption of 'mounting', the former was probably once 'briny'. But I hesitate to undo this charming accident.

[Additional stanzas from 1483 Mrs Elizabeth Smitherd (65) at Tewkesbury 1908:

I would roll you in my arms
My dearest Jewel
So stay at home with me
And don't be cruel.

She fell upon the ground
Like one that was dying
This house was full of grief
Sighing and crying

Farewell my dearest friends
Father and Mother
I am your only child
I have no brother

It's in vain to weep for me
For I am going
Into everlasting joys
Where fountains are flowing]

Another version of this affecting song appeared in the *Journal of the Folk-Song Society*, No. 3, 1901. It is very similar, and gives 'briny' for 'brandy'. In a later issue of the same publication, No. 11, 1907, A. G. Gilchrist suggested that the song had a literary origin, and Lucy Broadwood gave as its original a broadside entitled *The Welcome Sailor*. The tune was noted by Vaughan Williams and adapted to the well-known hymn by Bunyan, 'He who would valiant be'.

While probably nineteenth-century in its present form, it seems to have earlier roots. Mrs Smitherd's version confuses the original situation, transforming a naval expedition into a voyage to eternity. The song may have been converted to religious uses, as Sharp says the Salvation Army took over *O No John*, substituting the refrain 'Yes Lord'.

72 Our Goodman

(The Cuckold's Song)

Now it's my old man came home one night
Came home one night to me
A strange horse in the stable he found
What strange horse can this be?
What strange horse can this be my love
What strange horse can this be?
'Tis a milking cow his wife replied
My mother she sent to me
Many thousand miles I've travelled
Ten thousand miles or more
But a saddle on a milking cow
I never saw before

Now it's my old man came home one night
Came home one night to me
A strange pair of boots on the stairs he found
What strange pair of boots can this be?
What strange pair of boots can this be my love
What strange pair of boots can this be?
It's a milking pail his wife replied
My mother she sent to me
Many thousand miles I've travelled
Ten thousand miles or more
But spurs on a milking pail
I never saw before

OUR GOODMAN

Now it's my old man came home one night
Came home one night to me
And a strange hat on the stairs he found
What strange hat can this be?
What strange hat can this be my love
What strange hat can this be?
It's a chamber pot his wife replied
My mother she sent to me
Many thousand miles I've travelled
Ten thousand miles or more
But a fur all on a chamber pot
I never saw before

Now it's my old man came home one night
Came home one night to me
A strange coat on the bed he found
What strange coat can this be?
What strange coat can this be my love
What strange coat can this be?
It's a counterpane his wife replied
My mother she sent to me
Many thousands miles I've travelled
Ten thousand miles or more
But buttons on a counterpane
I never saw before

Now it's my old man came home one night
Came home one night to me
A strange man in the bed he found
What strange man can this be?
What strange man can this be my love
What strange man can this be?
It's a baby his wife replied
My mother she sent to me
Many thousand miles I've travelled
Ten thousand miles or more
But whiskers on a baby's face
I never saw before

OUR GOODMAN
[1005 James Brooks at Bridgwater 1906. One other version]
Stanzas 1 and 3 in reverse order in ms.

This song is of troubadour origin, and became popular in several languages. It appears among French ballads as *Marianne amd Le Jaloux*. It was known in England at least as early as the mid-eighteenth century. Child has Scottish and English versions, and it was given also by Bell (1857), and Baring-Gould (1890). Alfred Williams (1923) collected several versions in the Thames valley. All the versions are parallel but vary considerably in detail. Most conclude not with a whiskered baby but with a bearded milkmaid.

73 *Pery Mery Winkle Domine*

I had four sisters sailed across the sea
   Pery mery winkle domome
And each of them sent a present unto me
   Partrum quartrum paradise lostum
   Pery mery winkle domome.

The first brought a chicken without a bone
The second brought a cherry without a stone

The third brought a book that is not read
The fourth brought wool without a thread

How can there be a chicken without a bone?
How can there be a cherry without a stone?

How can there be a book that is not read?
How can there be wool without a thread?

When the chicken's in the egg it has no bone;
When the cherry's in the flower it has no stone;

When the book is in the press it is not read;
When the wool is in the fleece it has no thread.

PERY MERY WINKLE DOMINE

[3025 (Music) Miss Aimers at Stratford-upon-Avon 1914. No other version]
1.4–5 It is clear from the music that 'paradise' and 'domome' each have three syllables.

This is a version of the well-known medieval riddle song of the mid-fifteenth century or earlier, *I have a yong suster fer beyondyn the se* given in the Sloane ms. For a full discussion see *The Oxford Dictionary of Nursery Rhymes*, p. 387. It has been suggested, but without certainty, that the refrain is adapted from a Roman Catholic hymn or was a Latin exorcism. I have not seen the present version elsewhere. Partridge gives 'periwinkle' as a mid-nineteenth century low colloquialism for 'the female pudend'.

74 *Poaching Song*

When I was bound a prentice
In famous Somersetshire
I served my master truly
For nearly seven year
Till I took up to poaching
As you shall quickly hear
For 'twas my delight on a shining night
In the season of the year.

As me and my companions
Were setting of a snare
The gamekeeper was watching us
But for him we did not care
For we can wrestle and fight my boys
Jump over anywhere
It is my delight etc.

As me and my companions
Were setting four or five
In taking of them up again
We caught a hare alive
We popped her in the bag my boys
And through the woods did steer
For it's my delight etc.

POACHING SONG

We threw her across our shoulders
And wandered through the Town
And called into a neighbour's house
And sold her for a crown
We sold her for a crown my boys
But dare not tell you where
For it's my delight etc.

So here's success to poachers
For I do not think it fair
Bad luck to every gamekeeper
That will not sell his deer
Good luck to every landlady
That wants to buy a hare
It's my delight on a shiny night
In the season of the year.

[1480 Mrs Elizabeth Smitherd (65) at Tewkesbury 1908. Three other versions]

2.5 *wrestle and fight*: 1480 wrestle fight
3.2 *four or five*: 1480 for a five
5.4 *deer*: any game.
5.5 *landlady*: this is the only one among the many versions of this song, so far as I know, which refers to a landlady. Other versions wish good luck to 'gentlemen' and bad luck to 'magistrates'.

When Bell (1857) printed this song, he insisted that it properly belonged to Lincolnshire, and that the earliest text he had seen, of about 1776, named this county. Its popularity is indicated by its adoption in Somerset, Northamptonshire and Leicestershire. The risks involved in poaching, and the consequent excitement of the game, are illustrated in *Van Dieman's Land* (No. 107).

75 *Poor Nell*

It's of a wealthy lawyer in Southwark he did dwell
He had a handsome housekeeper and she was called Nell
He hugged and kissed her o'er and o'er as I for truth do tell
Till her apron grew too short before saying O poor Nell

POOR NELL

It happened on a certain night, as they were lying in bed
She wept she wailed she wrung her hands and furthermore she said
My Virgin rose you stole away, O wed me Sir, said she
Or I like unto other poor girl say O poor me.

He took her by the lily white hand and said my own sweetheart
Since you and I together have met I hope we never shall part
And if ever I offer to breach my vow as sure as Hell is Hell
I hope the Devil will fetch me and carry me to his cell.

So then with joys and pleasing toys they passed away the time
Till seven months were gone and past and two left out of nine
He turned her out of his service quite, as I for truth did tell
All for the sake of a lady bright, he left poor Nell.

One day as she was all alone lamenting her sad fate
A curious frolic come in her head, which made her laugh outright,
Says she: I'll dress myself as black as any devil in hell
I'll wait some night for his coming home saying O poor Nell

She straightway to a chimney sweeper went and there a bargain
    made
All for to have his sweeping clothes and furthermore she said
If thou for me my counsel keep here's a guinea I'll give to thee
And let thy little sweeping boy to go along with me.

She straightway learnt the boy his tale, these words to him did say
If thou wild act thy part right well here is a crown for thee
With a pair of ram's horns on her head in a lonesome place stood
    she
And as for black the sweeping boy sat under a tree.

Between the hours of twelve and one as you for truth shall hear
This lawyer he came trudging home from the courting of his dear
In steeping o'er to shun the dirt, as I for truth do tell
She nimbly caught him by the skirts saying O poor Nell.

And with a doleful hollow voice these words to him did say
According to the promise I made I'm come to take you away
You must away along with me down to my gloomy cell
Or else tomorrow by the break of day you wed poor Nell.

POOR NELL

With this the little sweeping boy set fire to a train
Which wrapt and cracked about his legs and made him roar amain
O master devil spare me now and mark well what I tell
Tomorrow by the break of day I'll wed poor Nell.

See that you do, the devil he said, and mark well what I say
You see my little devil sitting under yonder tree
And if ever you offer to break your vow as sure as hell is hell
That little devil shall fetch you and carry you to his cell.

The lawyer he went home in a most dreadful fright
And early next morning as soon as it was light
With staring eyes and trembling joints he looked most wondrous pale
He went to her with a humble voice good morning dear Nell.

With kisses and with compliments, he gained her consent
And having got the license unto the church they went
There he made her his lawful bride as I for truth do tell
And ever since live a happy life saying O Brave Nell.

She never told no friend nor foe the project she had played
Till nine months were gone and passed and she'd been put to bed
She told it to her gossipers which pleased them right well.
The husband laughed and smiling said Well done Brave Nell.

[648 Captain Lewis at Minehead 1905. Two other versions, one fragmentary]

Although I know of no other text of this, it is obviously a typical Georgian broadside. The narrative is direct and vigorous enough, but the padding-out of the lines with clichés like 'as I for truth do tell' and 'mark well what I do say' distinguishes the broadside from the true folk song. Folk songs have their own stock phrases, but these are seldom mere padding.

Although the 'lawyer' of this kind of ballad is interchangeable with 'merchant' or 'farmer', there is a distinctive 'lawyer' type in popular literature, recognizable again in *Mowing the Barley* (No. 64). He is amorous, loose-principled but good-humoured, and is always outwitted.

76 The Poor Old Couple

There was an old couple and they was poor
    Right fol lol diddle all dee
There was an old couple and they was poor
And they lived in a house that had but one door
      And poor folks was they
      And poor folks was they

Now the little old man he went from home
And he leaved this little old woman alone
    And that was hard said she

There was a town clerk who lived close by
And he was resolved with her to lie
    And that was kind said she

Now eight o'clock and a little o'er
A gentle knock came to the door
    Who is that said she?

O 'tis the town clerk O don't be afraid
Come down and open the door he said
    O yes I will said she

At twelve o'clock and a little o'er
Another knock came to the door
    Who is that said she?

It is your dear husband O don't be afraid
Come down and open the door he said
    O yes I will said she

Now fetch me an apple from yonder tree
And I will come and let in thee
    O yes I will said he

Now as he was a grabbling under the tree
Up jumped the town clerk and away runned he
    That's very well done, said she.

THE POOR OLD COUPLE

> O I have been sick since you have been gone
> My sickness was all for the want of a man
>   Poor wife said he
>   Poor cuckold thought she.

[1768   Henry Reed (83) at Axbridge 1908. Three other English versions and one American]
8.3   *he*: 1768 she

Sharp's other versions are parallel, except that in one the old man falls down the apple tree and dies, having been put to bed with his head tied up in blue ribbons.

It has been suggested that this song is related to *The Old Man Can't Keep his Wife at Home* (Baring-Gould, *Songs of the West*, 1890), which is based on the story of Tofano in the Decameron, but there is little connection. I can find no other version except a severely censored 'nursery song' communicated to Alfred Williams (*Folk-Songs of the Upper Thames*, 1923).

77 *Poor Old Horse*

A

> O once I was clothed
> In a linsey 'oolsey fine
> My mane it hung down
> And my coat it used to shine
> But now I'm growing old
> To dust I must decay
> My master ofttimes frowns
> One day I heard him say
> Poor old horse he must die
>
> You are old and you are cold
> Your pace it is but slow
> You eats all my hay
> And you breaks all my straw
> And neither are you fitten
> All in my team to draw
> We will whip him, cut him, skin him
> To the hounds we'll let him go
> Poor old horse, he must die.

POOR OLD HORSE

Now my flesh to the hounds
So freely will I give
My body to the huntsman
As long as I am to live
Besides those active legs of mine
That have run so many a mile
Over hedges and ditches
Over fancy gates and stiles.
Poor old horse, you must die.

Now nature's all over
I've done my best and worst
And all that they can do
Is to turn me into dust
And don't you think it's hard
To have to know disgrace
If I could see my time again
I would win the Derby race
Poor old horse, you must die.

B

When I was young and in my prime
And in my stable lay
They gave to me the very best corn
And the very choicest hay
Poor old horse, poor old mare!

My coat I'll give to my master
My shoes I'll throw away
The dogs shall eat the rotten flesh
And think how I will decay
Poor old horse, poor old mare!

My master rode me out
And tied me to a stile
While he was courting the miller's girl
While I could trot a mile
Poor old horse, poor old mare!

POOR OLD HORSE

Now I'm old and done for
Fit for nothing at all
I'm force to eat the sour grass
That grows along the wall
Poor old horse, poor old mare!

[A 2146 Charles Tanner (66) at Bampton 1909
B 105 Lucy White and Louie Hooper 1904]

A

Alfred Williams, in his *Folk-Songs of the Upper Thames*, 1923, gives two versions, of which one was taken down from Charles Tanner at Bampton, the source of A. This is the only instance I have seen of a song noted twice from the same singer by different collectors. There is no means of telling which version is the earlier. Alfred Williams' version, referred to below as AW, is almost identical, except that it unfortunately lacks the last stanza; and it enables me to clear up one or two confusions in Sharp's version.

1.2 *linsey 'oolsey*: linsey-woolsey, i.e. a mixture of linen and wool.
2.8 *To the hounds we'll*: emended from AW (2146 Till the hounds will)
3.4 *As long as I am to live*: AW For I'd rather die than live
3.8 *fancy gates*: AW fences, gates
4.5–8 2146:
(If I could see my time again)
And don't you think it's hard
To had to no disgrace
If I could pay myself again
I would win the Derby race
4.8 The Derby was first run in 1780.

Bell (1857) printed a version, and said it formed part of a mummers' play as acted at Richmond, Yorks. Lucy Broadwood (*Journal of the Folk-Song Society*, No. 5, 1904) said that in Nottinghamshire it was still used as part of a house-to-house performance, in which a man carried a horse's skull painted black and red. In these mummings the jaws of the skull were made to snap loudly in time to the words of the refrain. Bell and others stated that the play was of Scandinavian origin, and referred originally to Odin's Sleipnor. They give no evidence for this. Others connect it with the hobby-horse ritual in English morris dancing. Bell claimed that his was the first printed text, but Baring-Gould, who noted two West Country versions, pointed out that broadside versions existed earlier. Kidson scornfully rejected the theory of a Scandinavian origin, and other anthropological explanations, and called it 'purely a humanitarian view of the fate of old worn-out horses'.

It has been printed in many versions, and the extreme diversity of these suggests an ancient origin. The *Journal of the Folk-Song Society*, No. 3, 1901, p. 75, prints a text beginning 'I am a warrior', and containing the line 'A-chasing of those French dogs over five-barred gates and stiles'.

Sharp published in *Folk Songs from Somerset*, 1904, and *English Folk Songs*, 1921, Vol. II, a version based on 105 (B, above).

78 *The Rambling Boy*

In Kerry city I was born and bred
In Shipham's Green I died with scorn
I served my time at a saddling trade
I was always counted a roving blade

At seventeen I took a wife
I loved her dearly as I love my life
And to maintain her both fine and gay
I went a robbing on the highway

I robbed Lord Golding I do declare
Lord Mansfield at Clover Square
I shoot the shooters and bid them good night
And away I went to my heart's delight

To Fielding's Garden I took my way
With my blooming lass to see the play
Till Fielding's gang did me pursue
Taken I was by that cursed crew

My father cried for his darling son
My wife cried I am now undone
My mother she tore her white locks and cried
I wish that in his cradle he had died

Now when I am dead and going in my grave
A flashy funeral pray let me have
Let none but robbers all them follow me
Give them broadswords and sweet liberty

Get six pretty maidens to bear up my pall
Give them white gloves and white ribbons all
That they might say when they speak the truth
There's gone a wild and wicked youth

[1034 Joseph Laver at Bridgwater 1906. One other version]

1.1 *Kerry city*: 1034 kerry. 1672 Dunlin town (? Dublin)
1.3 *a saddling*: 1672 some sailor's
1.4 *roving*: 1672 roguish
2.4 *highway*: 1672 king's highway

THE RAMBLING BOY

3.2 *Clover Square*: other versions have Grosvenor Square
3.3 *shoot the shooters*: shut the shutters (*Journal of the Folk-Song Society*, No. 3, 1901, p. 114).
4.1 *Fielding's*: 1672 Cupid's
4.3 *Till*: 1672 Lord

6 and 7 are not in 1034 and are taken from 1672. Similar stanzas occur in other ballads, e.g. the American cowboy song, *The Streets of Laredo*.

The following splendid variant occurs in Sharp's ms. version of *Tarpaulin Jacket* (625 John Griffiths at Bridgwater 1905):

> And when that I'm dead and buried
> And passed through all troubles of life
> Let there be no more sobbing and crying
> But do a good turn for my wife
> Wrap me up in my tarpaulin jacket
> And fiddle and dance o'er my grave
> Let six jolly fellows all carry me
> And let them be terrible drunk
> And as they are going along with me
> O let them fall down with my trunk
> O there shall be such laughing and joking
> Like so many men going mad
> They shall take a glass over my coffin
> And say I'm a hearty true lad

This ballad must have been very popular to judge from the number of versions. These are parallel, but differ considerably in detail, especially place-names. The highwayman's birth-place is given variously as Kerry, Dublin, Newlyn and Newry. Covent Garden is a variant on Cupid's Garden. In some versions Stephen's Green is given instead of Shipham's Green, and in others the name of the highwayman is Charley Reilly. There is a strong probability of an Irish origin, though I am unable to identify the circumstances related.

79 The Red Herring

O what do you think I made out of my red herring's head
I made so good oven as ever baked bread
So it's beagles and long dogs and a man to whip in
And don't you think I done well with my jolly red herring?

O what do you think I made out of my red herring's tail?
I made so good ship as ever set sail
So it's etc.

THE RED HERRING

O what do you think I made out of my red herring's ribs?
Made forty new cradles and fifty new cribs
So it's etc.

O what do you think I made out of my red herring's guts?
I made so good dreshuls as ever dreshed woats
So it's etc.

O what do you think I made out of my red herring's navel?
As good an old put as ever drained gravel

O what do you think I made out of my red herring's whole
I made as good wagon as ever hauled coal
So it's etc.

[448 Mrs Hooper 1904. Four other versions, including fragments]
4.2 *dreshed woats*: threshed oats (dreshul is a dialect term for a threshing implement).
6.1 *whole*:? hole

Sharp published a somewhat different text in Novello's *School Songs*, 1909. The song was also noted by Alfred Williams (*Folk-Songs of the Upper Thames*, 1923).

80 *The Rigs of London Town*

From London Town I went astray
'Twas in Oxford City that I lost my way
The finest girl that I did meet
She treated me with kisses sweet.
 He's up to the rigs, he's down to the rigs
 He's up to the rigs of London Town

She took me to some house of fame
The sign of the Ship in Water Lane
A roaring supper she did call
Thinking I should pay for all

THE RIGS OF LONDON TOWN

Now when supper was over and table clear
She calls me her jolly and a roving dear
She calls for wine both white and red
And a chambermaid to make our bed.

Now between the hour of one and two
She asked me if to bed I'd go
And I therewith I gave consent
And up to the bedroom door I went

When this fair maid got fast asleep
Slowly from her I did creep
I stole her watch her silken gown
Her gold rings and twenty pounds.

Now come all you young men wherever you be
When you meet with a lass that is jolly and free
You use her well, I doned the same
But remember the Ship in Water Lane

[1473 Henry Barrett (61) at Randwick 1908. One other version]

1.5 *rigs*: tricks. (The ms. has Rigs for the second rigs.)
2.3 *roaring*: riotous.
A version of this song with minor variants was noted by E. J. Moeran in Norfolk in 1924. (*Journal of the Folk-Song Society*, No. 35, 1931.)

81 *Rosemary Lane*

A

I lived in service in Rosemary Lane
I keep the good will of my master and dame
Till a sailor came there one night for to lay
And that was the beginning of my misery

ROSEMARY LANE

He called for a candle to light him to bed
And likewise a silk handkerchief to tie up his head
To tie up his head as he used for to do
Says he pretty Polly will you come to bed too?

The girl being young and foolish she thought it no harm
To jump into bed to keep herself warm
But what was done there I'll never declare
But I wish that short night had been seven long year

'Twas early next morning this sailor arose
And into her lap throw handfuls of gold
Saying this I will give and more I will do
If you'll be my Polly wherever I go

When your baby is born you put it to nurse
And set like a lady with gold in your purse
With gold in your purse and milk in your breast
Saying that's what you've got by your sailor in the West

And if it's a boy he shall fight for his King
And if it be a girl she shall wear the gold ring
She shall wear the gold ring and her top knot shall blow
Saying that's what you've got by your Sailor true blue.

B

A drowsy young soldier he hung down his head
And asked for a candle to light him to bed
She handed him a candle her duty it was to do
And when she got inside the room she asked him in bed too
   My own dearest home is my own countree
   My own dearest home is my own countree
   The ivy and the oak and the bonny willow tree
   Is all growing green in my own countree

She jumped into bed to keep his back warm
Thinking that the soldier would do her no harm
He huddled her and cuddled her and called her all his dear
He wished that short night had been seven long years
   My own dearest home etc.

ROSEMARY LANE

Now if it's a boy he shall wear a gold ring
And when he's of age he shall fight for his King
And his jacket so red and his trousers so blue
He shall fight for his country like his father used to do
    My own dearest home etc.

Now if she's a girl she shall wear a gold brooch
With silver in her pocket and gold in her purse
With silver in her pocket to buy milk and bread
And you may depend she'll never trust a soldier in her bed.
    My own dearest home etc.

Now all you young girls a warning take by me
Never trust a soldier one inch above your knee
For I trusted one and he disappointed me
And went away and left me with a baby on my knee.
    My own dearest home etc.

[A   459 Mrs Overd 1904. Two other versions
B   1403 Mrs Florence Chedgy at Stackland 1908. One other English and one American version]

A
  6.2 *wear the gold ring*: i.e. get married and be a lady.

B
    4 and 5   These are replaced by the following in 27 Louie Hooper and Lucy White at Hambridge 1903:
    If it is a girl she shall stay at home with me
    And if it is a boy he shall cross the raging sea
    With his low gaitered boots and his jacket so blue
    He shall stand upon the deck like his Daddy used to do

    When you have a baby you put it out to nurse
    And sit in your chair with gold in your purse
    With gold in your purse and milk in your breast
    And to see what you're coming to by a sailor in the West.

Sharp did not publish this, but a version was printed in the *Journal of the Folk Song Society*, No. 21, 1918. B appears in Sharp's ms. under the title *The Oak and the Ash*, but the only connection is in the refrain. Lucy Broadwood says the song was a stock broadside, and it is possible that the Oak and the ash' refrain became attached to it in this way.

82 *Rout of the Blues*

As I crossed over Salisbury Plain
But a dainty fine sight I behold
As lasses were crying and tearing their hair
O the rout is just come for the Blues

Then each one home to their mothers did run
My heart is undone it is true
I'll pack up my clothes without more delay
And boldly I'll march with the Blues

The Landlord and Landlady walks hand in hand
And so do they pretty girls too
Then each one poured out a bottle of gin
To drink a good health to the Blues

Our ship she's been rigged and we all set sail
How sweetly the French Horn played too
And they each of them gave a loud Huzza
Success to King George and his Blues.

[2179 Tom Gardiner (71) of Blackwell at Armscote 1909. One other version]

Rout of the Blues: Marching Orders for the Foot Guards.
3   289 Mrs Louie Hooper 1904:
   The Landlords and ladies are troubled in mind
   And so are the young women too
   For to see the young lasses go down in the boats
   For to take their farewell of the Blues, the Blues
   For to take their farewell of the Blues.

Versions of this occur on broadsides. The usual place-name variants appear, such as 'Scarborough Sands', 'down King Street one day', for 'Salisbury Plain'.

83 *The Rover*

I am a rover and that's well known
I'm just a going to leave my home
Leaving my home and my friends to roam
Farewell my bonny lass till I return.

O I set myself down and I wrote a song
I wrote it wide and I wrote it long
At every line O I shed a tear
And at the end of every verse 'I've lost my dear'.

O am I married or am I free
O am I bound for to married be
A married life you soon shall see
A contented mind shows no jealousy.

As I crossed over yon Belsimore
There I lost sight of my true love's door
My heart did ache my eyes went blind
When I thought of the bonny girl I left behind.

I wish I wish but it's all in vain
I wish I was but a maid again
A maid again O I never shall be
Till an apple grows on an orange tree.

[660   Rober Dibble at Bridgwater 1905. One other version]

335   Mr Bullen at Ilchester 1904 has the following additional stanza but is otherwise parallel:
I wish I wish 'twas all in vain
I wish my love would return again
Return again he never will more
For he died at sea where the billows roar.

This is somewhat incoherent, and the 'I wish I wish' stanza occurs elsewhere. The song seems to consist of stanzas from some longer original in which there are two speakers, a man and a girl.

84 The Roving Journeyman

I am a roving journeyman
I travel the country round
When I come near London Town
I'm willing to sit down
With a kit all on my shoulder
The trowel in my hand
When I come to London Town
I'm willing to sit down

One treat me with the bottle
Other treat me with the can
Let the toast go round my boys
Unto the journeyman.
I hadn't been in London Town
But one or two or three
Before my master's daughter
Growed very fond of me

She asked me in to dine with her
She took me by the hand
She slyly told her mammy
She liked the journeyman.
No, hold your tongue dear daughter
How can you say so?
To fall in love with a country lad
You never seen before.

Hold your tongue dear Mammy
I'll do the best I can
And tomorrow night I'll go to bed
Along with the journeyman.

[170   Abraham Laurence at Ilminster 1905. Three other versions]

This song is given in a more literary form by Baring-Gould (*Songs of the West*, 1890), who says there are inferior broadside versions. The occupation of the journeyman in Sharp's version is that of a mason or bricklayer; but for 1.6 Baring-Gould has 'A grafting knife in hand'.

85 *The Sailor and the Soldier*

A sailor and a soldier was a walking one day
Said the sailor to the soldier I've a mind for to pray
Pray on said the soldier pray on once again
And pray for whatever thou wilt I will answer Amen

The first thing they came to was an old hollow tree
Said the sailor to the soldier this my pulpit shall be
Pray on said the soldier pray on once again
And pray for whatever thou wilt I will answer Amen

The first thing I'll pray for I'll pray for our King
That he have peace and plenty all the days of his reign
And where he got one man I wish he had ten
And never never want an army Said the soldier Amen

The next thing I'll pray for I'll pray for the King
That he have peace and plenty all the days of his reign
And where he got one ship I wish he had ten
And never never want for Navy said the soldier Amen.

The next thing I'll pray for is a pot of good beer
For good liquors were sent our spirits to cheer
And where we got one pot I wish we had ten
And never never want for liquor, said the soldier Amen.

[2032 William Stokes (66) at Chew Stoke 1909. One other version]

Published by Sharp in the *Journal of the Folk-Song Society*, No. 18, 1914, and in *Folk-Songs from Various Counties*, 1912.

86 *Sailor Cut Down in his Prime*

His good old father, his aged mother
Oft times had told him of his past life
Along with those flashy girls his money he'd squander
Along with those flashy girls was his delight.

Now he is dead, and laid in his coffin
Six jolly sailor boys walk by his side
Each of them carried a bunch of white roses
That no one might smell him as he passed by.

At the corner of the street where stood two girls talking
One to the other would whisper and say
Here comes a young sailor whose money we squander
Here comes a young sailor cut down in his prime

On the top of the tombstone these words are written
All you young fellows take warning by me
Never go courting the girls of the city
The girls of the city was the ruin of me.

Beat the drum over him, play the pipe merrily
Play the dead march they carries him on
Take him to the Churchyard and fire three volleys over him
It was a young sailor cut down in his prime.

[109 Mrs Mary Bunstone at Hambridge 1904. No other English version]

2.4 *by*: 109 bye

The sailor is evidently the victim of venereal disease, and the significance of the flowers may be as a disinfectant. I have found no other published text, but a number of versions are to be found in ms. collections and journals of limited circulation, under such titles as *St James' Hospital* and *The Unfortunate Rake*. In the two versions Sharp collected in America the narrative is sentimentalized. Compare this funeral with that described in *The Rambling Boy* (No. 78). The *Journal of the Folk-Song Society*, No. 17,1913, contains a companion piece, *The Young Girl Cut Down in her Prime*. The cause of her death is even more obscure, but her obsequies are much the same.

87 *Sailors they are such a Sort*

Sailors they are such a sort
They gets a gallant sweetheart in any port
For they are so gallant so careless and wild
They do not care for wife nor for child
So do not you marry with a sailor or then
For they're ranting roaring wild young men

Landsmen they have money for to lend
But what a sailor gets he always spends
He runs like a madman when he gets on shore
Drinking all night and home with his whore.

O mother dear mother then what should we do?
If it weren't for the sailor that ploughs the ocean through
We all would be sailors' if they had the heart
So I intends to take some gallant sailor's part
For I loves a sailor as dear as my life
And intends to be some gallant sailor's wife.

Daughter dear Daughter since I had known your mind
To some gallant sailor your heart it is inclined
You go and get married as soon as you can
All the money I have shall be at your command
For I have been told the very most of them
Are clever genteel smart young men.

[939 William Mead at Bridgwater 1906. No other version]
  2.4 *whore*: 939 w . . . e

The singer's memory was evidently defective, but I have found no printed text with which to compare Sharp's ms.

88 *Salisbury Plain*

As I rode over Salisbury Plain
'Twas there I met a scamping-lie young blade
He kissed and enticed me so
Till along with him I was forced for to go

SALISBURY PLAIN

At length some public house we came at last
And there for man and wife we did pass
Who called there for ale wine and strong beer
Till to bed together we both did repair

Undress yourself my darling said he
O come, O come in bed along with me
O that won't do my darling said she
You'll keep all those flash girls away.

Those flash young girls you need never to fear
For you shall be safeguarded my dear
I'll maintain you like a lady so gay
If I go robbing all on the high way.

So early next morning my love rose
Immediately he put on his clothes
All on the high way he set sail
He robbed both the coaches and the mail.

It's now in Newgate cells my love lies
Expecting every moment to die
May the Lord have mercy on his poor soul
For I think I heard his death bell toll.

All young men a warning take by me
Never let no flash young girls gain your heart
For if that you do you will rue
And die on the high drop at last

[1523 Mrs Mommery at Shipley 1908 (learnt from an old man 80 years old, named Propley, who lived at Copyhold, Shipley, 53 years ago: Sharp's note) No other version]

   1.2 scamping-*lie young blade*: highway robber.
   2.4 *repair*: 1523 appear
   7.1-2 In 1523 'men' and 'girls' are transposed.

The above reading is in accordance with the only other printed text, that noted by Vaughan Williams (*Journal of the Folk-Song Society*, No. 8, 1906). This is similar to Sharp's version, but omits stanzas 2, 3 and 4.

89 *The Sea Captain*

It's of a sea captain who was married of late
'Twas to a young lady and he gained her estate
He was a sea captain and bound for the sea
But before she was bedded he was called away.
      And sing Fal the dal al the dal day

There was a young Squire who lived near by
And went to this lady resolved to try
Saying the Captain your husband he is gone from home
I'll make him a cuckoo before he return.

Then early next morning the Squire arose
He dressed himself in the best of his clothes
With his coachman and footman and butler so fine
He goes to the lady and bids her be kind.

Upstairs the young lady with the Squire did go
The cook and the coachman did follow also
The housemaid and footman all in the next room
And the butler all night in the garret with Joan.

All night they did sport and when daylight was come
There was fifty pounds offered for daughters or sons
And then said the squire I'll vow and declare
I have fathered a score this very same year.

When six months were over and seven were past
The slender young lady grew thick in the waist
When eight months were over and nine they were gone
That very same night the Captain came home.

He took her in his arms and he gave her a kiss
Saying my dearest jewel you're thick in the waist
'Tis nothing but fat, love, the lady did say
Would you have me grow slender when you are at sea?

THE SEA CAPTAIN

When supper was ended they sat in the hall
This slender young lady she gave a loud squall
The colic, the colic, the colic she cried
I'm so bad in the colic, I'm afraid I shall die.

The doctor was sent for and when he came there
He ordered the cook some drink to prepare
The cook then she answered all in the same room
I'm so bad in the colic I cannot come down

The midwife was sent for and when she came there
She delivered the lady of a beautiful heir
She delivered the cook and then with the same
The housemaid and Joan made an end of the game.

O then said the captain there's fun I declare
But for the joke's sake I forgive you my dear
But there's one thing more pray tell me if you can
If these four babies were got by one man?

[653 Captain Lewis at Minehead 1905. (Got in an old book, written in fly leaf. Heard and learned tune from an old man in Porlock Weir: Sharp's note.) No other version]

90 *Searching for Lambs*

As I walked out one May morning
One May morning betimes
There I behold my own true love
Just as the sun did shine.

The birds of Love so sweetly did sing
How fragrant was the air
There's none but her, but her alone
Among the lilies fair

What makes you stroll abroad so soon
Your journey to pursue
Before bright Phoebus glorious shine
To strike off the morning dew.

SEARCHING FOR LAMBS

I'm going for to feed my father's flock
His young and tender lambs
They're over hills and lonesome rocks
Lamenting for their dames.

As we sat under the myrtle shade
How the little lambs did sport and play
And unto him these words did say
My dear and only Jay.

How glorious like the sun do shine
And pleasant was the air
But I'd rather be in my true love's arms
Than any other where.

If you should stroll away my Love
No man could comfort me
For I am thine and thou art mine
And a married we will be.

[732 James Bishop at Hunter's Lodge, Priddy 1905. Five other versions, one fragmentary]

A composite text mainly from 732 with additional lines from 1003, 925, 1295 and 2040.

    3.3 1003 Your pretty little feet they tread so sweet. I have retained the 'Phoebus' line from 732 in spite of its literary flavour, because it preserves the classical metaphor complete—that of the sun-god ravishing the flowers at dawn by drying up the dew of virginity (see pp. 54–55). Moreover, it is possible that the word 'feet' has been adapted from 'Phoebus'.
    4.3 *lonesome rocks*: 2040 shady groves, 1003 over dales
    5.1 *myrtle*: symbol of faithful love.
    6.1 *glorious like*: 1003 gloriously
    7 The final stanza varies somewhat from one version to another. A variant used by Sharp in his text is: 'We'll join our hands in wedded bands.'

Sharp published a text in *Folk Songs from Somerset*, IV, 1909, and again in *English Folk Songs*, Selected Edition, 1921, Vol. I. In his note in the latter he says: 'So far as I know, this has not been published elsewhere. . . . Taking words and tune together, I consider this to be a very perfect example of a folk-song.'

This is one of the very few folk songs containing biblical imagery. See *The Song of Songs*, VI, 3: 'I am my beloved's, and my beloved is mine: he feedeth among the lilies.'

91 *The Seeds of Love*

I sowed the seeds of love,
'Twas early in the Spring,
In April and May, and in June likewise,
The small birds they do sing.

My garden is well planted
With flowers everywhere,
But I had not the liberty to choose for myself
Of the flowers that I loved dear.

My gardener he stood by,
I asked him to choose for me;
He chose me the violet, the lily and the pink,
But these I refused all three.

The violet I forsook
Because it fades so soon.
The lily and the pink I did overlook
And I vowed I'd stay till June.

For in June there's a red rosebud,
And that's the flower for me,
So I pulled and I plucked at the red rosebud
Till I gained the willow tree.

For the willow tree will twist
And the willow tree will twine,
I wish I was in a young man's arms
That once had this heart of mine.

My gardener he stood by,
And he told me to take good care;
For in the middle of the red rosebud
There grew a sharp thorn there.

I told him I'd take no care
Until I felt the smart.
I pulled and I plucked at the red rosebud
Till it pierced me to my heart.

THE SEEDS OF LOVE

I locked up my garden gate,
Resolving to keep the key,
But a young man came a-courting me
And he stole my heart away.

My garden is over-run
No flowers in it grew,
For the beds that was once covered with sweet thyme
They are now over-run with rue.

Come all you false young men
That leave me here to complain
For the grass that is now trodden under foot
In time it will rise again.

[3359 Joseph Alcock at Sibford Gower, Warwickshire 1922. Thirteen other versions, including three fragments]

  3.3 *violet*: symbol of modesty.
       the lily and the pink: purity and courtesy.
  5.1 *red rosebud*: passion.
  5.4 *willow tree*: sorrow in love.
  9.2 *to keep the key*: remain a virgin.
10.3 *thyme*: hope.
       rue: repentance.

This was the first song that Sharp collected (see Introduction, p. 7). The version given here was noted much later. I have preferred it for its greater fullness. It appeared in one form or another in numerous ballad and song collections from the early nineteenth century onward, e.g. Bell, *Ballads and Songs of the Peasantry of England*, 1857; Kidson, *Traditional Tunes*, 1891; Lucy Broadwood, *English County Songs*, 1893. It was stated by Bell and others to have been composed by Mrs Fleetwood Habergam of Habergam, Lancashire, about 1689; but it seems more likely that she simply wrote down the song from the singing of others. It sounds much earlier than the late seventeenth century, and indeed, with its 'garden of love' and its flower-symbolism, its origin must be medieval.

Some editors, for example Kidson, have held, and others—for example, Sharp—denied, that the song is the same as another usually called *The Sprig of Thyme*. In any case, the two are, as Baring-Gould says, 'so mixed up together' that it is now impossible to disentangle them. It may be that in *The Seeds of Love* the prevailing mood is one of self-pity untinged with any blame for the seducer, while in *The Sprig of Thyme* there is an element of blame. But I cannot be sure about this; any attempt (such as those made by Baring-Gould and Sharp) to reconstruct a complete *Sprig of Thyme* would necessarily be tentative.

THE SEEDS OF LOVE

Sharp printed the first six stanzas of the above from a closely parallel version in *Folk Songs from Somerset*, I, 1904, and *English Folk Songs*, Selected Edition, 1921, Vol. I.

As in most songs where there are a number of versions, and where the lyrical element is stronger than the narrative, different versions disagree about the order of the stanzas, and about the elements included and omitted. *The Seeds of Love and The Sprig of Thyme* are bewilderingly rich in variants. I append a number of variant stanzas from Sharp's ms.

[1645   George Say at Axbridge 1908]
   He sowed on his garden full of seeds
   And the small birds they carry it away
   In April May and in June likewise
   When the small birds sing all day all day

[1218   Henry Thomas at Chipping Sodbury 1907]
   My garden it is run wild
   For the want of planting it new
   The beds that used to be covered with thyme
   Are all run into rue.

   Now I'll lock the garden gate
   And 'tis all for to keep the key
   Till some young man came with his flattering tongue
   And stole my time away

[471   Mrs Overd 1904]
   O once I had plenty of Thyme
   I could flourish by night and by day
   Till at length that saucy young man by chance came this way
   He stoled all my time away

[1407   Mrs Jarrett (54) at Bridgwater 1908]
   It's good to be drinking of beer
   Much better to be drinking of wine
   It's better to be sleeping in your own true lover's arms
   I wish I was sleeping in mine

[1353   Isaac Perkins (73) at Nettlebridge 1907]
   O the willow willow tree will twist
   And the willow willow tree will twine
   I wish I was in that poor girl's arms
   That stole away the heart of mine

   Now forsake all fading flowers
   And beware of false young men
   For it's give to me the girl that was trodden underfoot
   Give her time she will rise up again

92 *The Sentry*

As I walked out one evening
One evening on the strand
There I behold of a soldier
On Sentry he did stand.

He kindly saluted me
Which made me pass a joke
He took me into his sentry box
Rolled me up in his soldier's coat.

He keeped me there all that long night
Till daylight did appear
The soldier rose put on his coat
Saying fare thee well my dear

O soldier gallant soldier
Will you but marry me?
O no, my dearest dear
For children I have three.

Two wives I've got in the army
But one is too many for me
And if it wasn't for that my dearest dear
I'd quickly marry you.

[696 Thomas Hendy at Ilminster 1905. No other version]

This is clearly a poor relation of *The Bold Grenadier*, B, No. 17. It is very similar to a song noted by A. G. Gilchrist and printed in the *Journal of the Folk-Song Society*, No. 19, 1915, under the title of *The Gentleman Soldier*.

93 Sheep-Stealer

There was a sheep stole from the marsh
Will Marpass was the sinner
He stole the sheep last Saturday night
For Sunday for his dinner
So good a cook he had
She was so good and clever
For a very good pie we should have had
If she had got the liver.

A famous scratch we had
With the stuff we stole just now
We killed the sheep and skin 'un
Upon an open bough
One said he'll have the breast
Another said he'd have the chain
Said Wrestling Ned to Stumpy Jack
You'll tear off all the spine.

[1303 Mrs Wardberry at Ash Priors 1907. No other version]
   2.1 *scratch*: fight, dispute.
   2.6 *chain*: chine.

These vigorous stanzas are probably a fragment of a broadside ballad. I can discover no other text. Incomplete as they are, I print them in the hope of bringing the rest to light.

94 The Sign of the Bonny Blue Bell

As I was a-walking one morning in Spring
To hear the birds whistle and the nightingale sing
I heard a fair damsel so sweetly sung she
Saying I will be married on a Tuesday morning.

I stepped up to her and thus I did say
Pray tell me your age and where you belong
I belong to the Sign of the Bonny Blue Bell
My age is sixteen and you know very well.

Sixteen pretty maid you're young to be married
I'll leave you the other four years for to tarry
You speak like a man without any skill
Four years I've been single against my own will.

THE SIGN OF THE BONNY BLUE BELL

On Monday night when I goes there
To powder my locks and to curdle my hair
There'll be three pretty maidens awaiting for me
Saying I will be married on a Tuesday morning.

On a Tuesday morning the bells they shall ring
And three pretty maidens so sweetly shall sing
So neat and so gay is my golden ring
Saying I will be a-married on a Tuesday morning.

On Tuesday night when I goes to bed
With my precious jewel that I lately wed
Farewell and adieu to my maidenhead
Good night pretty maidens till Wednesday morning.

[33 Louie Hooper and Lucy White at Hambridge 1903. No other version]

1.3-4 Ms. indicates that these two lines are repeated as a refrain.
3.1 *you're*: 33 your
3.2 *for to*: 33 to be
3.4 *single*: 33 omits. Words supplied from Sharp's texts.
4.3 *There'll be*: 33 There was

Sharp published this in the *Journal of the Folk-Song Society*, No. 6, 1905, in Novello's *School Songs, Folk Songs from Somerset*, I, 1904, and *English Folk Songs*, Selected Edition, 1921, Vol. I, in all cases omitting stanza 6, and with other minor alterations. It was also noted by E.J. Moeran in Norfolk (*Journal of the Folk-Song Society*, No. 35, 1931). Kidson said it was on a nineteenth-century broadside, but it is obviously much older. Songs and dance-tunes with titles similar to the words of the refrain 'I will be married on a Tuesday morning' appeared in eighteenth-century collections.

95 *Single Men's Warning*

Come all you young men that are going to be wed
Don't be trapped like a bird with a small bit of bread
I'd have you be careful in choosing of a wife
O, for when you are trapped you remember it through life
   With fol di diddle di do, fol di diddle day

O when that you are wed and a squaller it is born
A poor man may work his fingers to the bone
He hears a midwife and a nurse, and a gossiping crew
And a poor man can hardly pull himself through

SINGLE MEN'S WARNING

When I go home to breakfast, to breakfast at eight
The devil of a spark of a fire in the grate
And the turk of a sign of a breakfast for me
And my wife she lay a snoring like a pig all in the stye

If I asked her to rise, she'd fly in a pet
And bawl out by God there's time enough yet
Get the breakfast thee self and be off to thee work
Don't bide here for to idle and lurk.

When dinner time come to home I repair
And a hundred to one if I find my wife there
She's gossipin' about with the child upon her knee
And the turk of a sign of a dinner for me.

When I go home at night sadly tired from my work
When I open the door she'll let fly like a Turk
Take the squalling young brat and get him off to sleep
For all the day long no peace I can get.

O but if I should offer the job to refuse
With the tongs and the poker she will me abuse
And if these are the comforts attending of our life
Good luck to the man that has got such a wife

And O if I could be but single again
The finest of ladies should never me trepan
Single I'd remain all the days of my life
Good luck to the man that has got such a wife

[101   Tom Sprachlan at Hambridge 1903. No other version]
Sharp did not publish this, and I have been unable to discover any printed text. There are of course many songs on the same theme, but this has a note of genuine feeling not always found and a refreshing lack of facetiousness.

96 *Still Growing*

The trees that do grow high, and the leaves that do grow green
The time is gone and past my love when you and I have seen
One cold winter's night my love when you and I alone had been
The bonny lad is young but he's growing

STILL GROWING

O father, O father, you have done me some wrong
You have married me to a bonny boy and you know he is too young
O it's daughter, dearest daughter, if you'll only wait a while
O a lady you shall be when he's done growing.

I'll send him to the college for one year or two
And perhaps in the time my love he then will do for you
We'll buy him white ribbons to tie all round his bonny waist
To let the ladies know that he's married

I went unto the college and I peep-ed over the wall,
I saw four and twenty young gentlemen, they was playing at bat and ball
I enquired for my own true love but they would not let him come
All because he was a young man a-growing.

Now at the age of seventeen O he was a married man
And the age of eighteen he was the father of a son
At the age of nineteen he was a-laying low
And the green grass was a-growing all over him.

At the age of twenty-one, O me and my son
We came into a large salary what the father he had won
We have to weep for the father because he's laying low
And the green grass growing over him.

I made my love a shroud of the fine holland brown
And every stitch I put in it the tears they will run down
And then I'll sit and mourn his fate until the day I die
But I'll watch all o'er his child while it's growing.

For now my love is dead and in his grave doth lie
The green grass was growing over him so very high
Saying once I had a sweetheart but now I have never a one
For he was to me my own true love for ever.

   [1446 Alfred Emery (78) at Othery 1908
  3341 Mrs Kathleen Williams at Puddlebrook Herefordshire 1921]
     (Three other English versions, and one American)
    2.2 3341 You have made me get married to a young man, and you know I am too young
    3.1 *I'll send*: 1446 I sent
    5.3 *nineteen he*: 3341 nineteen of age O he

This song and its many variants have been traced to a Scottish original based on historical fact, the marriage of Urquart of Craigston to Elizabeth Innes, and his death in 1634. This is highly speculative; in any case the folk song versions are well removed from their supposed originals. Early marriages for motives of material advantage were at one time common; in other versions the boy's age at marriage is given alternatively as 12 and 16.

The earliest text is in Johnson's *Scots Musical Museum*, 1792. Other collectors who published versions are: Lucy Broadwood, Frank Kidson and S. Baring-Gould. Sharp's ms. versions are defective and in places confused. He published a regularized text in *Folk Songs from Somerset*, I, 1904, and in *English Folk Songs*, Selected Edition, 1921, Vol. II; but I have preferred to give a text combining two ms. versions, with an essential minimum of emendation.

97 *Sweet Primaroses*

As I walked out one midsummer's morning
To view the fields and to take the air
'Twas down by the banks of the sweet primaroses
When I beheld a most lovely fair

Three long steps I stepped up to her
Not knowing her as she passed me by
I stepped up to her thinking for to view her
She appears to me like some virgin bride

I said pretty maid, how far are you going
And what's the occasion of all your grief
I'll make you as happy as any lady
If you will grant me one small relief.

Stand off, stand off, you are deceitful
You are deceitful young man, 'tis plain
It's you that have caused my heart to wander
And to give me comfort, it's all in vain

I will go down in some lonesome valley
Where no man on earth shall never me find
Where the pretty little small birds do change their voices
And every moment blows a blustrous wind.

SWEET PRIMAROSES

Come all young men that goes a-courting
Pray give attention to what I say
There's many a dark and cloudy morning
Turns out to be a sunshine day.

[171 John Edbrook at Bishops Nympton 1904. One other version]

  1.3 *primaroses*: traditionally associated with wantonness, as in Ophelia's advice to Laertes, and the Porter's speech in *Macbeth*.
  2.2 *knowing*: recognizing.
  2.4 *virgin*: 26 Virtue's
  5.3 *do*: 171 to

This was at one time common in broadsides and song collections. Sharp gives a slightly altered text in *Folk Songs from Somerset*, I, 1904, and in *English Folk Songs*, Selected Edition, 1921, Vol. I.

98 *The Tailor by His Trade*

I am a tailor by my trade
In buttoning up I am quite handy
And all the money I do earn
My drunken wife lay out in tea and brandy
    Right fal lal la la deet lal lal
    Fal la la la laddie.

O! If I go to seek a friend
Or for to take a noggin
My drunken wife she follows me
A cursing like a dragon

Saying come along home you drunken sot
Don't get spending all my riches
For you protect what you have got
And I will wear the breeches.

One night I sat down
Contented by the fire
She flinged the tea pot at my head
Which made me to retire.

THE TAILOR BY HIS TRADE

My wife was taken very ill
All in a week she died
I pretended myself to be very sad
But the devil for she I cried!

And now she's dead where is she gone?
She'll break no plates and dishes
And now she's dead and her tongue lies still
She must wear the wooden breeches.

[73 Tom Sprachland at Hambridge 1903. No other version]
  1.2 *buttoning up*: keeping my mouth shut, not complaining.
  6.4 *the wooden breeches*: the coffin.

99 *There was an Old Woman or The Rich Old Lady*

There was an old woman in our town
In our town did dwell
And she loved her husband dearly
But another man twice as well
    Whip she larey tidifoo larey
    Whip she larey O.

Now she went and got six marrow-bones
And she made him suck them all,
And that made the old man blind
Till he couldn't see any at all.

He swared he go and drown himself
If he could find the well
The old woman quickly answered:
O I'll show you the way.

She led him to the water
And took him to the brim.
And he said he'd drown himself
If she would push him in.

THERE WAS AN OLD WOMAN

The old woman she went to give a run
To push the old man in,
And the old man nimbly popped aside
And the old woman tumbled in.

She plunged about in the water
A -thinking she could swim,
But the old man went and got a puthering prop
And he propped her further in.

The old woman being gone to the bottom
And could no more be seen
The old man he went laughing home
And gained his sight again

So there's an end to my Song, Sir
And I can sing no more
And they that say that I can sir
Be a liar and son of a whore.

[3347   Mr Taylor at Ross Workhouse 1921
675   Mr Warren at Haselbury Plucknett 1905]
    (No other version)

  2 *Now she went and got* . . . 675 has the following defective stanza:
    She went unto the doctor
    To see what she could find
    You get some dozen o' marrow
      (last line missing)

  6.3 *puthering prop*: puther is a dialect word for stir.

  8.3 *whore*: 675 w—r. 3347 replaces this stanza by:
    So now my song is ended
    You may pen it down in ink
    I won't bother my head to sing any more
    If you don't give me some drink.

A composite text consisting of stanzas from both of Sharp's versions. Both are clearly defective, but I have not discovered the song elsewhere, nor the reason for the sub-title. The significance of the marrows or marrow-bones is obscure. It may be that she asked the doctor for a medicine to produce blindness and was given something harmless, whereupon the husband, being a party to the doctor's deception, made use of it to his own advantage and feigned blindness.

100 *The Thrashing Machine*

It's of a farmer near London 'tis said
He kept a servant a blooming young maid
Her name it was Molly, she was scarcely sixteen
She would work very well at the thrashing machine
    Fal di ral fal di dee

O Molly said Master, the times are hard
Will you go with me into the farmyard
You harness young Dobbin, you know what I mean
I think we can manage the thrashing machine
    Fal di ral fal di dee

O Master, says Molly what will Missus say
Never mind, says Master, she's making of hay
And while she is spreading the grass that is green
We can be working the thrashing machine
    Fal di ral fal di dee

So the barn doors were open, young Dobbin stood inside
The farmer got on the machine for to ride
O Master, says Molly, you think very clever
I think we can manage the thrashing machine
    Fal di ral fal di dee

So young Dobbin got tired of going round
He hangs to the traces, he bows to the ground
Altho' once in good order, he's now got a wen
Through working so hard at the thrashing machine
    Fal di ral fal di dee

O Molly says smiling we have had a loss
I think it requires a much stronger horse
If Dobbin was strong as before he has been
I think Why we would keep working the thrashing machine
    Fal di ral fal di dee

THE THRASHING MACHINE

Six months it passed over and truth for to tell
Molly's front parlour began for to swell
And that shortly after she had got her wean
The fruits of her labour with the thrashing machine
    Fal di ral fal di dee

[165 William Nott at Meshaw 1904. One other fragment]

  4.1 *inside*: 165 and sighed
  4.4 *thrashing*: 165 threshing
  5.3 699 O once in good order, but now thin and lean
  7.1 *and truth for to tell*: interpolated—line in ms. ends at 'over'
  7.3 *wean*: 165 wen

Sharp's unpublished ms. appears to be the only source for this song. The suggestion in the third stanza is that the farmer has already been cuckolded.
    The threshing machine would have been topical during the early years of the nineteenth century. According to the *Encyclopaedia Britannica* (14th edition), 'A workable threshing machine was invented late in the eighteenth century and was gradually coming into use early in the nineteenth; it was driven by water or wind power, sometimes by horse labour, and later by steam. But it was not until the '30s of the nineteenth century that steam began to be applied at all extensively to agriculture.'

101 *The Three Cripples*

Three cripples from London on the spree
Once came down to the counterie.
They eat and drank three down or more
And then they said there was somebody there.

And when the time for bed did come
They called the waiter into the room.
And one said: Here, take charge of my eyes.
The other says: Here, lay these teeth by.

THE THREE CRIPPLES

The waiter ran downstairs in a fright
And told his master with all his might.
Lord, said he, if you had but upstairs have been,
And seen the sight which I have seen.
They're pulling out arms, legs like fun
And unscrewing legs O one by one.

They sent for a parson to come and pray
To try to send them all away.
But nothing wouldn't do till a soldier came;
They didn't vally him nor his name.

The soldier he smiled through the spree
And he went and told the company.
He told them if they'd go away
Their shots were all settled and there was nothing to pay.
They screwed on their legs and they hopped away.

[3356   Fred Webb at Bloxham, Oxon 1922. No other version]

  4.4   *vally*: value (3356 bally)

This appears to be an imperfect recollection of an early nineteenth-century song based probably on an eastern tale. I have not discovered any other version.

102 *Three Maids a Milking*

Three maids a milking did go
Three maids a milking did go
The wind it did blow high, the wind it did blow low
And it wavèd their pails to and fro

They met with some young man they knew
They met with some young man they knew
And they asked of him if he had any skill
In catching a small bird or two.

THREE MAIDS A MILKING

O yes I have very good skill
O yes I have very good skill
O it's come along with me to the yonder green wood
And I'll catch you a small bird or two.

Away to the green woods they went
Away to the green woods they went
And they tapped at the bush and the bird it did fly in
And it flew just above her lily white knee

Here's a health to the bird in the bush
Here's a health to the bird in the bush
For the birds of one feather they will all flock together
Let the people say little or much.

[1207   William Stokes at Chew Stoke 1907. Three other versions]
   1.4   *wavèd*: 1207 wai-ved

   4   1163
      Away to the yonder green 'ood
      Away to the yonder green 'ood
      Where they all bait their birds and the young it flew in
      And then they'd a bird of their own

   5.2   1475 Let it be a blackbird or thrush

   1475   has the following additional stanza:
      Here's a health to our king on his throne
      Here's a health to our king on his throne
      For we'll drink down the sun, and we'll tarry till the morn
      And we'll drink to our neighbours and friends

A version of this was the last song Sharp collected. He published no text, but a similar version was given in the *Journal of the Folk-Song Society*, No. 15, 1910. This was slightly edited, as was that in *Folk-Songs of the Upper Thames* (Alfred Williams, 1923). Baring-Gould (*Songs of the West*, 1890) gives a modified and confused text, and refers to a nineteenth-century broadside version. This is presumably the one published in *The Common Muse* (Pinto and Rodway, 1957), which is fuller than any other version.

This is evidently a song transferred to broadside literature from oral tradition. The sexual symbolism, somewhat confused by modern singers, and obscured altogether by some editors, points to an early date. 'Milking pail' and 'milk' as symbols of the female sexual organ and semen respectively are traceable at least to the seventeenth century. While this may be a seventeenth-century convivial song, I am inclined to think it is of earlier origin.

103 *Three Maids a Rushing*

Three pretty maidens a rushing they went
And a rushing was their intention.
One proved by child before they did return
And she rolled it underneath her apyrin.

O Sally come home with her heart full of woe
                    and her eyes full of tears
What is the matter with you my daughter dear
And what have you got under your apron.

Father O father dear father said she
It's only my new gown and that's too long for me
And I'm afraid it will draggle driggle dree
And I rolled it underneath my apron.

In the dead of the night when all were fast asleep
Then this little baby began for to weep
What a little dicky bird have you got singing there
In the chamber amongst the pretty maidens.

Father O father dear father said she
It's a little baby more sweeter than me
Let it lie, O let it lie this night along with me
I will tell you its daddy in the morning

Is it by a black, or is it by a brown
Or is it the gentleman belongs to London Town
That give to you the stranger to wear with your new gown
And you rolled it underneath your apyrin.

It's neither by a black and it's neither by a brown
It was by the sailor boy that sails from London Town
That give to me the stranger to wear with my new gown
And I rolled it underneath my apyrin.

[1580 Jack Barnard at Bridgwater 1908. One other version, confused and fragmentary]
   2.2 Line incomplete in ms.

This unpublished ms. is the only source I have discovered of what is evidently part of a ballad of some antiquity. The questioning of the daughter by the father is strongly reminiscent of *Lord Thomas of Winesberry* (No. 59).

104 *The Tree in the Wood*

(In each of these two versions of the well-known cumulative song the opening stanza is printed first. At each succeeding repetition a fresh line is added, until the final stanza, printed below, is reached.)

A

There was a tree grew in the wood
The findest tree that ever was seen
The tree grew in the wood
And the green leaves growed all around around around
And the green leaves growed all around.
. . . . . .
There was a tree grew in the wood
The findest tree that ever was seen
The tree grew in the wood
The limb grew on the tree
A branch grew on the limb
A nest was on the branch
An egg was in the nest
A yolk was in the egg
A bird was in the yolk
A wing was on the bird
A feather was on the wing
And the green leaves growed all around around around
And the green leaves growed all around.

B

In the Merryshire woods there growed a tree
And a very fine tree was he
And the tree growed in the Merryshire wood
In the Merryshire wood in the Merryshire wood
And the tree growed in the Merryshire wood.
. . . . . .

THE TREE IN THE WOOD

In the Merryshire woods there growed a tree
And a very fine tree was he
And on that tree there was a limb
And on that limb there was a branch
And on that branch there was a spray
And on that spray there was a nest
And in that nest there was an egg
And in that egg there was a bird
And on that bird there was a feather
And on the feather there was a bed
And on that bed there was a maid
And on that maid there was a man
And the tree growed in the Merryshire wood
In the Merryshire wood in the Merryshire wood
And the tree growed in the Merryshire wood.

[A   845   Mrs Grace Coles at Enmore 1906
B   746   John Vincent at Priddy 1905]
   (Two other versions)

A

2.8 Line interpolated from 1346 (as in most versions)
Music Book 3068 has the following conclusion:
   A feather was on the wing
   A colour was on the feather
   O this colour it was blue.

Sharp printed a text of this song similar to A in *Folk-Songs from Somerset*, IV, 1908, in *English Folk Songs, Selected Edition*, 1921, Vol. II, and *Novello's School Songs*, 1908. Parallel texts are given in *English County Songs* (Lucy Broadwood, 1893) and in *Folk-Songs of the Upper Thames* (Alfred Williams, 1923). The *Journal of the Folk-Song Society*, No. 13, 1909, printed part of a version similar to A, concluding with the words 'The rest is wanting'. In her notes to this A. G. Gilchrist refers to Breton, Danish, Swiss and Welsh versions, and to a 'Very polite' French nursery version. This implies that Sharp's B version is nearer to the source than any other hitherto printed. Still more complete, however, is a version noted, but never published, by Baring-Gould (Ms. No. CIV). Here, after the stanza about the maid, a 'lad' sleeps with the maid, a baby is begotten, from the baby grows a boy, and the boy plants an acorn, the acorn becomes a tree, and the circle is completed. This explains the title by which the song is sometimes referred to—*The Everlasting Circle*.

105 *The Turtle Dove*

Farewell my joy and heart's delight
I must leave you for a while
If I go away I will come again
If I go ten thousand miles my dear
If I go ten thousand miles.

Ten thousand miles it is too far
To leave me here alone
Here I may lie lament and cry
Thou cannot hear my moan my dear
Thou cannot hear my moan.

Your moan my dear I cannot hear
Your case I cannot cure
If I go again I will come again
When all your friends are pleased my dear
When all your friends are pleased.

Suppose my friends will never be pleased
And look with an angry eye
O then I will love thee more and more
Until the day I die my dear
Until the day I die.

O don't you see that milk white dove
Sitting on yonder green tree?
Lamenting for her own true love
As I lament for thee my dear
As I lament for thee.

You call me where you see me not
And speak by me as you find
And don't be like the weather weather cock
That changes with the wind my dear
That changes with the wind.

The crow that is so black my dear
Shall change his colour white

THE TURTLE DOVE

If ever I prove false to thee
The day shall turn to night my dear
The day shall turn to night.

[679 per Miss Kitty Sorby from Enmore 1906. Five other English versions, three of them fragmentary, and seven American versions]

1.1 *my*: 879 for
4.4 1640 Until the seas run dry my dear
6.1 This line is obscure and possibly corrupt. It becomes clearer if we take 'call' to mean 'recall' or 'call to mind'. The general sense of this and the next line would thus be: 'Think of me in my absence, and don't be influenced by the slanders of others.'

5 568 has:
Can't you see the little turtle dove
Setting under the mulberry tree
See how she do mourn for her true love
And I shall mourn for you

7 1640 has:
The crow that flies so very high
Shall change his colour to white
If ever I prove false to my own true love
Bright day shall turn to night my dear
Bright day shall turn to night

This ms. also has the following additional stanza, following Stanza 4 in 679:
Suppose the sea should never run dry
Nor the rocks never melt with the sun
Then you and I will never never part
Until these things are done my dear
Until these things are done.

The following is an interesting American variant from 2372 Mrs Reuben Hensley at Carmen, North Carolina 1916:
O don't you see yon little turtle dove
A -skipping from vine to vine
A -mourning the loss of its own true love
Just as I mourn for mine.

Don't you see yon pretty little girl
A -spinning on yonder wheel,
Ten thousand gay, gold guineas would I give
To feel just like she feels.

This song made its way from oral tradition into broadside literature, and was also used by Burns in the composition of *A Red, Red Rose*. The versions noted by modern collectors vary considerably as to the elements included or omitted. The above text is fuller than any other I have seen. Sharp printed partly abridged, composite texts in *Folk Songs from Somerset*, II, 1905, and *English Folk Songs*, Selected Edition, 1921, Vol. I.

106 *The Two Jovial Butchers*

It's of two jovial butchers
As I have a heard men say
They both of them took five hundred pound
All on a market day.

As they were jogging homeward
Together side by side
Says Johnson unto Nelson
I hear some woman cry.

They searched the woods all over
Till a woman they behold
And she was stripped stark naked
And exposed to the cold.

Young Johnson he being a valiant man
And a man of courage bold
He took his coat from off his back
To keep her from the cold.

He took her up behind him
And carried her a little ways
Till she put a whistle to her mouth
Which made a dismal noise.

And through the woods came roving blades
With weapons all in their hands
They came up to young Johnson
And bid him for to stand.

I'll stand, I'll stand says Johnson
I'll stand as long as I can stand
For I never was in all my life
Afraid of any man.

THE TWO JOVIAL BUTCHERS

So young Johnson beat the seven of them
And the rest he did not mind
Till this cruel hearted woman
Took a knife from her side and ripped him up behind.

And now she is in prison
Bound down with iron strong
For killing of the finest young butcher
That ever the sun shined on.

[55 Tom Lynes at Bredon, Puckington 1903. One other version and one fragment]

  3 2107 has an additional stanza and a variant:
I will not stop said Nelson
I will not stop said he
I will not stop said Nelson
For a robbed we shall be.

Then Johnson he got off his horse
And searched the woods all round
And there he found this woman lie
With her hair pinned to the ground

  6.1–2 2107:
Then up came three young swaggering blades
With their staves all in their hands

Fuller texts were published by Lucy Broadwood (*English Traditional Songs and Carols*, 1908) and Alfred Williams (*Folk-Songs of the Upper Thames*, 1923). These and Sharp's versions are evidently abridged from broadsides, of which the earliest appears to be a black-letter copy of 1678 in the Roxburghe *Ballads*. There are more frequently three than two butchers, and their names are Ips, Gips and Johnson, or Gibson, Wilson and Johnson. The robbers vary in number from three to ten, and are armed with staves, swords or pistols, according to the date of the version.

107 *Van Dieman's Land*

Come all you gallant poachers
That rambles devoid of care
That walketh out on a moonlight night
With dog and gun and snare.
Here's the hares and lofty pheasants
They stands at your command
But you don't think on the dangers
All on Van Dieman's Land.

Here's poor Tom Brown from Nottingham
Jack Williams and Poor Joe
They was three of the daring poachers
The Country did well know
One night they was trap-handed
By the Keeper hid in sand
And for fourteen years transported
All on Van Dieman's Land.

The very first day we landed
All on that fatal shore
The planters they came round us
About three score or more
So they harnessed us up like horses
And fit us out of hand
And they yoked us to the plough my boys
To plough Van Dieman's Land.

O those wretched huts that we live in
Is built with clods and clay
And rotten straw for bedding
We dare not to say Nay.
Our cottages they're all fenced with fire
We slumber whilst we can
To drive all wolf and tiger
All from Van Dieman's Land.

One night all in my slumbers
I had a pleasant dream
I dreamed I was with my dear wife
Down by some purling stream

VAN DIEMAN'S LAND

With the children's prattling stories
All around me they did stand
But I awake quite broken hearted
All on Van Dieman's Land.

Here is a girl from Nottingham
Susan Somers is her name
She got fourteen years transported
For selling of our game
But the planter bought her freedom
And married her out of hand
And she proved true and kind to us
All on Van Dieman's Land.

[1120 Robert Parish at Exford 1906. No other version]

- 2.5 *trap-handed*: trepanned, i.e. ensnared.
- 3.6 *fit*: other texts have 'sold'.
- 6.4 All other versions have either 'We all well knew the same' or 'For playing of the game'
- 6.5 *planter*: 1120 planters

Sharp did not publish this broadside ballad, but full versions are given in the *Journal of the Folk-Song Society*, No. 4, 1902, in *English Traditional Songs and Carols* (Lucy Broadwood, 1908), in *Folk-Songs of the Upper Thames* (Alfred Williams, 1923) and in *The Common Muse* (Pinto and Rodway, 1957).

Van Diemen's Land was first colonized by British settlers in 1797. The name Tasmania does not appear to have come into general use until after the first quarter of the nineteenth century.

108 *Waly Waly*

Down in the meadows the other day
Gathering flowers both fine and gay
Gathering flowers both red and blue
I little thought what love can do

Where love is planted there it do grow
It buds and blossoms just like some rose
For it has a sweet and a pleasant smell
No flower on earth can it excel.

WALY WALY

I put my hand into the bush
Thinking the sweetest flower to find
I pricked my finger to the bone
And leaved the sweetest flowers alone.

I leaned my back up against some oak
Thinking it was a trusty tree
First he bended then he broke
And so did my false love to me

There is a ship sailing on the sea
But it's loaded so deep as deep can be
But not so deep as in love I am
I care not whether I sink or swim.

Love is handsome Love is pretty
Love is charming when it's true
As it grows older it grows colder
And fades away like the morning dew

Must I be bound and he go free
Must I love one that don't love me
Why should I act such a childish part
To love a man that will break my heart

[989   James Thomas (89) at Connington 1906
604   Mrs Caroline Cox at High Ham 1905
504   Elizabeth Mogg 1904
1027   Elizabeth Mogg at Doddington 1906]
    (No other English versions, one American)

The above is a composite text using stanzas from the four English versions. All the stanzas not included in this text are as follows:

8   The water is I (*sic*) wide I can't get over
    Neither have I got wings to fly
    Go and get me O some little little boat
    To carry over my true love and I

9   I had two dogs under my father's table
    They do prick their Ears when they do hear the horn
    When I'm dead dear it will be all over
    And I hope my friends will bury me

WALY WALY

10 In London city the girls are pretty
    Streets as paved with marble stones
    My true love the clever a woman
    As ever trode on English ground

11 I'm often drunk but seldom sober
    I'm a rover in every degree
    When I'm drinking I'm always a thinking
    How to gain my love's company

12 Since my love's dead and gone to rest
    I'll think on her who I love best
    I've sewed her up in flannel strong
    Have another now she's dead and gone.

Assuming the stanzas of the composite text to be numbered 1 to 7, the four versions are made up as follows (with minor variations in the stanzas common to more than one version):

　989　(Thomas) 1, 2, 4, 7
　604　(Cox) 1, 3, 4, 5, 12
　504　(Mogg 1904) 8, 6, 9
　1027　(Mogg 1906) 8, 10, 11,9

Note. In Stanza 7 the ms. (989) gives 'she' for 'he' in Line 1, and 'girl' for 'man' in Line 4. Since the protagonist is obviously feminine—Stanza 4 alone proves this—I have, for the sake of consistency, adopted this reading from the version noted in 1905 by H. E. D. Hammond and printed in the *Journal of the Folk-Song Society*, No. 27, 1923. Singers were often inconsistent about nouns and pronouns denoting sex, especially in non-narrative songs.

(For a full account of this song see Introduction, pp. 38–40.)

109 *Well Done Liar*

I saw a snail drive a nail
Well done Liar
I saw a snail drive a nail
Give him his due
I saw a snail drive a nail
From Penzance up to Hayle
Isn't that a comical thing to be true

WELL DONE LIAR

I saw a wren kill a man
Well done Liar
I saw a wren kill a man
Give him his due
I saw a wren kill a man
With a dag in his hand
Isn't that a comical thing to be true

I saw a maid milk a bull
Well done Liar
I saw a maid milk a bull
Give him his due
I saw a maid milk a bull
Every stroke a bucket full
Isn't that a comical thing to be true

[2983 (Music) Mr Tom Thomas (65) at Camborne 1914. (Learnt this when a boy from a very old woman: Sharp's note.) No other version]

   2.6 *dag*: 2983 gives the gloss '(hatchet)', but surely an abbreviation for 'dagger'.

These unpublished stanzas are probably a convivial song of Anglo-Irish origin. Partridge (*A Dictionary of Slang and Unconventional English*, 1937) gives for 'wren': 'a harlot frequenting Curragh Camp, military 1869'; for 'dew': 'whisky: Anglo-Irish 1840' (evidently a pun is intended in Line 4); and an Irish origin for 'kill' meaning to defeat or exhaust. One of the meanings of 'milk' in the same source is 'cause sexual ejaculation'.

110 *When shall we get Married*

O when shall us be married
To my old dear Nickety Nod
I think on Sunday morning
And won't it be wonderful good.

And who shall us ask to the wedding
My old dear Nickety Nod
I think father and mother
And won't it be wonderful good

WHEN SHALL WE GET MARRIED

And can't we ask nobody else
To my own dear Nickety Nod
What think we can ax the Queen and her guards
Methinks the girl is mad

And what shall us have for our breakfast
To my old dear Nickety Nod
And I think bacon and eggs
And won't it be wonderful good

Can't us think nothing better than that
To my old dear Nickety Nod
Think we can have roast baked and boiled?
Methinks the girl is mad

And when shall us go to bed
To my old dear Nickety Nod
What thinks we can go and leave all the volks here?
Methinks the girl is mad!

And when shall us have some children
To my old dear Nickety Nod
And when please God to send 'em
And won't it be wonderful good

And what thinks we can have 'em before we have made 'em?
Methinks the girl is mad

[1394 Elizabeth Frost (79) at Upton Pynes 1908. Three other versions]

Three of the ms. versions are indexed under the title *Nickety Nod*. 1739 gives the name as 'Nickledy Cod'. At the end of the above version are the words 'They then dance'. The song appears to have been connected with a dance which was also popular among children. Variants are found in song collections from the eighteenth century onwards, but there are signs of considerably greater age. Halliwell's text (1846) names the man 'Nicholas Wood', and contains the punning line 'Why, sure the man's gone wood!' The medieval sense of 'wood' was 'mad'. It is used in this sense in *A Midsummer Night's Dream* (II 1.192) but was uncommon by Shakespeare's time.

111 *Whistle Daughter Whistle*

Mother I longs to get married
   I longs to be a bride
I longs to lay by that young man
   And close to by his side
Close to by his side
   O happy should I be
For I'm young and merry and almost weary
   Of my virginity.

O daughter I was twenty
   Before that I was wed
And many a long and lonesome mile
   I carried my maidenhead
O mother that may be
   It's not the case by me
For I'm young and merry and almost weary
   Of my virginity.

Daughter daughter whistle
   And you shall have a sheep
I cannot whistle mother
   But I can sadly weep
My maidenhead does grieve me
   That fills my heart with fear
It is a burden a heavy burden
   It's more than I can bear.

Daughter daughter whistle
   And you shall have a cow
I cannot whistle mother
   For 'deed I not know how
My maidenhead does grieve me
   That fills my heart with fear
It is a burden a heavy burden
   It's more than I can bear.

WHISTLE DAUGHTER WHISTLE

Daughter daughter whistle
  And you shall have a man
  (*whistles*)
You see very well I can
You nasty impudent Jane
  What makes you whistle now?
O I'd rather whistle for a man
  Than either sheep or cow.

You nasty impudent Jane
  I'll pull your courage down
Take off your silks and satins
  Put on your working gown
I'll send you to the fields
  A tossing of the hay
With your fork and rake the hay to make
  And then hear what you say.

Mother don't be so cruel
  To send me to the fields
Where young men will entice me
  And to them I may yield
For mother it's quite well known
  I am not too young grown
For it is a pity a maid so pretty
  As I should lay alone.

[869 Walter Locock at Martock 1906. One other version]

1.8 *my virginity*: 715 my poor virginity
2.5 *may be*: 869 may
5.5–8 These lines do not occur in the ms., but as the stanza is defective they have been supplied from the printed text (see below).
5.5 *Jane*: in the printed text Sharp gives 'jade', but I have retained 'Jane' from 869 as the word was commonly used for a pert girl.

Sharp's collections appear to be the only source for a full version of this song, which recalls a well-known German dialect folk song. An emended text was printed in *Folk Songs from Somerset*, III, 1906, and in *English Folk Songs*, Selected Edition, 1921, Vol. I, with the following note: 'The words given me by the singer were a little too free and unconventional to be published without emendation, but the necessary alterations have, nevertheless, been very few and unimportant.'

A three-stanza nursery version in *The Oxford Dictionary of Nursery Rhymes* (1951) is there stated to have a ms. original dated 1740.

112 *The Wife of Usher's Well*

There was a lady in merry Scotland
And she had gone by three
She sent them into merry England
To have some English teen

They had not been in Merry England
Past twelve months and one day
Before she had news from her three sons
They was clothed in cold clay.

She would not believe in God, she said,
Nor Christ nor the Trinitee
Except they would send her three sons back
Safe as they went from she.

They sent her three sons back
They sent her three sons back
You must put life into their bodies
Their bodies into a chest
Their bodies into a chest

And when they got to their own mother's gates
They knocked as they got to their own mother's gates
There was no one so ready as their own sweet mother
To let these sweet souls in
To let these sweet souls in

Sin their cloth was spread, the meat was set
No meat O Lord can we eat
No meat O Lord can we eat

Why don't you eat dear children she said
Why don't you make some cheer
Since has it been ever so long
Since we have seen you before

THE WIFE OF USHER'S WELL

How can we eat dear mother they said
How can we make any cheer
When you would not our sweet souls rest
At Heaven when we were there.

Up did crow the milk white cock
And then did crow the red
And ain't that a pity they all three said
As the quick shall part from the dead.

They ta'en a high yew tree by the top
And splored it by the root
And ain't that a pity they all three said
As the quick should part from the dead.

Farewell stick and farewell stone
Farewell to the maidens all
Farewell to the nurse that gave us suck
And down the tears did fall.

[2795 (Music). Sent to me by Miss Blunt, from the Vicar of Swerford near Hook Norton, Oxon 1912. One other English version and twelve American]

    1.1 *merry Scotland*: the only instance I know of this epithet so applied.
    1.4 *teen*: 3321 dee. The meaning is obscure. All American versions give the following (or a variant of it): 'To learn the grammaree' (i.e. reading and writing, or just possibly magic).
    2.3–4 In the American versions the cause of death is given as 'sickness'.
    4 This stanza is very corrupt: in a parallel Shropshire version printed by Child the corresponding stanza is part of an appeal to Jesus of which the third line is: 'And put breath in their breast'.
    7.2 and 8.2 *cheer*: MB 2795 cheer(s)
    8.3–4 In the American versions and the Shropshire text cited above it is made quite clear that the wife is guilty of a deadly sin in demanding her sons back from death.
    10.2 *splored*: tore up.

Corrupt and garbled as this is, I have included it because it is very different from the version generally accepted, and because it is an instance of the ultimate fate of the medieval ballad in the south of England.

113 William Taylor

I'll sing you a song about two true lovers
And from Lindsfield town they came
And the young man's name was William Taylor
And the young woman's name was Sarah Jane

William Taylor's a nice young sailor
He went courting a lady gay
And just as he was going to be married
Pretty William went to sea

So she dressed herself in man's apparel
Man's apparel she put on
And she's gone to seek her own true lover
For to find him she is gone

One day as she was exercising
All exercising with the rest
Her silver buttons flew off her waistcoat
And the captain beheld her milk white breast

Then the captain stepped up to her
And asked her what brought her there
I'm come to seek my own true lover
Whom I lately loved so dear.

If you are come to seek your true love
Pray tell me what his name may be
She cried his name is William Taylor
From the Irish ranks came he

You've come to seek your own true lover
And he hath proved to you severe
For he is married to a rich young lady
He was married the other year

WILLIAM TAYLOR

You rise early tomorrow morning
You rise by the break of day
There you shall see your true love Billy
Walking with some lady gay

She rose early the very next morning
She rose early the break of day
There she saw her William Taylor
Walking with a lady gay.

And then she called for a brace of pistols
A brace of pistols she did command
So she bide and shoot her William Taylor
With his bride at his right hand

And then our captain was well pleased
He was well pleased what she had done
Soon she became a bold commander
Over the captain and his men.

[257 Frederick Crossman at Huish 1904
21 Louie Hooper and Lucy White at Hambridge 1903
849 Mrs Pike (per Mrs Snow) at Somerton 1906
2027 William Stokes (66) at Chew Stoke 1909]
    (Two other English and three American versions)

1.2 *Lindsfield*: a broadside version gives 'Lichfield'
2. In 21 this stanza is replaced by the two following:
William Taylor was a brisk young sailor
He who courted a lady fair
The bells are ringing, sailors singing,
And to church they did repair

Thirty couple were their wedding
They were dressed in rich array
'Stead of William being married
He was pressed and sent to sea.

3.4 This line is missing in the mss. and has been supplied from Sharp's printed texts.

WILLIAM TAYLOR

4   In 849 this stanza is replaced by:
   She dressed herself in man's apparel
   Went to fight among the rest
   The winds did blow her jacket open
   There they saw her lily white breast
and in 257 the third line is replaced by: A silver locket fell from her bosom
4.1   *she*: 257 they
5.4   In 257 this line is replaced by: For he hath proved to me severe
10.1   In 849 this line is replaced by: She for a sword and pistol ordered
11   In 257 this stanza is replaced by the following two:
   Now this captain was well pleased
   Was well pleased with what she'd done
   So she soon became a beau-commander
   On ship board with all his men.

   Then the captain was well pleased
   Was well pleased with all that passed
   It was only three weeks after
   Sarah became the captain's wife.

This is a composite text consisting of all the elements in Sharp's ms. versions, none of which is complete by itself. Sharp published a version in *Folk Songs from Somerset*, V, 1909, Novello's *School Songs*, 1910, and *English Folk Songs*, Selected Edition, 1921, Vol. I, consisting essentially of Stanzas 2, 3, 5, 6, 8, 9, 10 and a concluding stanza whose origin is obscure.

This ballad was always a favourite, and was noted all over Britain. The main outline of the story is the same in all versions, but there is a bewildering variety of minor variations.

It is not at all clear that the original 'William Taylor' was a sailor. There is strong evidence that he was a soldier: some versions mention no naval activities whatever, but in fact contain specific military details. It is possible that both a naval and a military version existed and were sometimes confused, as in Sharp's versions.

Whatever his profession, it seems possible that William Taylor actually existed, since his name never changes, unlike those of the heroine and of his birthplace.

Was he already married to the 'lady gay' when courting Sarah? If so, did he deliberately run away to sea in order to escape the impending bigamy? The press-gang, it should be noticed, occurs only in some versions.

These uncertainties do not seem to have troubled singers or their audiences, and the song was adopted by polite society, and introduced into theatre programmes 'with great applause' during the later eighteenth century.

114 *Willie's Courtship*

As Willie came by his love he did cry
'Tis hazy weather, hazy weather
Yes Yes it is so and home I must go
For the clouds do gather, clouds do gather.
Clouds, the clouds do gather

O no no no you must not go
You look so pretty, look so pretty
Pretty poo poo! but I know who
Is vastly witty, vastly witty
Vastly vastly witty!

Then he took out his knife for to end his life
His love thus proving, love thus proving.
And by Gemini stars, indeed and it was
Most vastly moving, vastly moving
Vastly, vastly moving.

O Willie she cried I will be your bride
I only was foolish, only foolish
But to come for to go for to frighten me so
It was vastly foolish, vastly foolish.
Vastly vastly foolish.

[1973 Sister Emma (71) of Clewer 1909. No other version]

I have included this as an example of the oddities Sharp discovered amidst genuine folk poetry, and because it is possibly a unique copy.

115 *Young Barnswell*

Abroad as I was walking
All on one summer's day
I heard two lovers talking
These words to him did say

YOUNG BARNSWELL

O true love, true love Samuel
I'm come to break my vow
O, true love, true love, Saro
Don't tell me nothing so.

My friends and brother Barnswell
Are in such spite with thee
Swearing that they will slay thee
All on the mountains high

Your friends and brother Saro
Take me for such a man
But not them do I care for
I'll do the best I can.

Give to me your hand sweet Saro
And stand you true by me
And I will fight young Barnswell
All on the mountains high.

And when you're on the mountains
You're by yourself alone
You're far from town or city
You're far from any home.

You're far from town or city
Where no one will come by
Pray use my brother kindly
All on the mountains high.

Young Barnswell spoke to young Samuel
Saying 'Tis unto me draw nigh
'Tis here I mean to slay thee
All on the mountains high.

Young Samuel stood amaz-ed
Not knowing what to say
And at last stepped up to him
And took his bow away.

YOUNG BARNSWELL

His arrow he took from him
His bow he slent in three
There, he cried out, young Barnswell
I have no shot for thee

And yonder he spied young Saro
She's tripping all over the plain
Thinking to meet her brother
And her true love being slain.

Young Barnswell he stepped up to her
And took her by the hand
And gave her to young Samuel
In the place where they did stand.

May God send you prosper both
All the days of your life
I give you my dear sister
To be your wedded wife

I must confess that you
Were a better man than I
It lay in your power to slay me
All on the mountains high.

[78. Mrs Laurence at Somerton (per Miss Snow) 1906. No other version]
1   An obviously garbled stanza which may not belong here at all.
3.1   *brother Barnswell*: 780 brother, Barnswell. It is clear that Barnswell was the brother of Saro.
3.2 and 3.3   *thee*: 780 me
4.1   *brother*: 780 brothers
12.1–2   780 has only one line here: Young Barnswell took her by the hand. I have supplied the words He stepped up to her (cf. 9.3) to complete the stanza.
13.4   *wife*: 780 life

The only published text I have been able to trace appears under the title *Captain Barniwell in Folk-Songs from the Upper Thames* by Alfred Williams (1923). This version differs from Sharp's in a number of details. There is no counterpart in the standard ballad collections (e.g. Percy and Child). I do not know what to make of it. Feeble as it is in some respects, it shows genuine ballad traces; but whether it is a true ballad debased or a defective 'literary' imitation is a nice question.

APPENDIX

I. Fragments of unidentified folk-songs, evidently authentic.

(a) Have you seen my love pass by
With her cheeks like the roses
Or have you heard my love is married
Then I wish them both much joy
Although they do not hear me

[270 Mrs Welch at Hambridge 1904]

(b) It's how can I be merry and free
Or in my mind contented be
The bonny young lad I love so dearly
He is banished quite out of my company.

Kissing is a silly thing
It'll bring poor lovers into sin
I wish I was in the young man's arms
I'd care not whether I sink or swim

[452 Mrs Welch 1904]

(c) O 'twas of one summer's morning
Before it was got light
The cuckoo she sat singing
And the stars they gave no light
When they all told me my love was quite gone away
And how shall I get married
S [t] aying no not I
Since my heart has grown so heavy
Since my Love has gone away

APPENDIX

> I hugged her I kissed her
> Till she had changed her mind
> She changes with the weathercock
> She changes with the wind
> And how shall I get married
>
> (I rumpled up her chin)

[1144 William Crockford at Bratton 1906]

2. The following are given as examples of literary or sophisticated pieces adopted into the popular repertoire. Despite superficial resemblances, they are as easily distinguishable from true folk songs as the 'cowboy' and 'hill-billy songs purveyed in Hollywood and New York are distinguishable from their American prototypes.

(a)

Logan's Bright Water

> The red moon is up on the moss-covered mountain
> The hour is at hand when he promised to roam
> It's my aye bonny Mary bright stars of Llangary
> She's health and she's wealth and a good wife to me.
>
> Still she's the blossom I'll wear in my bosom
> A blossom I'll wear and wear till I die,
> It's my aye bonny Mary bright stars of Llangary
> She's health and she's wealth and a good wife to me.
>
> Along comes the Miller with plenty o' siller
> Logan's bright water she's a turf-cutter's daughter
> It's my aye bonny Mary bright stars of Llangary
> She's health and she's wealth, yes, and a good wife to me

[45 Louie Hooper and Lucy White at Hambridge 1903]

APPENDIX

(b)

Sweet Jenny of the Moor

One morn for resurrection as I strayed by the sea-side
The sun was gently rising bedickt in all his pride
I beheld a lowly maiden sitting at the cottage door
With bloom in her cheeks sweet Jenny of the moor.

I stared in complexion and viewed its charming sands
And filled with admiration methinks a fairy dream
Enchanted by that fair one as she walked along the shore
Gathering choice sea weed, Sweet Jenny of the Moor

I said my pretty fair one why so early do you rise
I love to greet the morning air when the larks soar in the skies
The spot is sweet to wander by though the breakers often roar
And wakes the bosom of the deep said Sweet Jenny of the Moor

We both sat down together by the pleasant shady side
And I said my dear with your conscience I will make you my bride
I've a plenty of my own command brought from the foreign shore
And proud's the man that wins the hand of Sweet Jenny of the Moor

[1708 Amos Ash, 50, at Combe Florey 1908]

(c)

A Sweet Country Life

A sweet country life is most pleasant and charming
All for to walk abroad on a fine Sumber's morning
Bright Phoebus did a-shine and the hills was adorning
As Molly she set a milking on a fine Sumber's morning

APPENDIX

No fiddle nor flute nor Hautboy nor spinnut
Is not to be compared with the lark nor the linnut
Down as I did lie all among the green rushes
'Twas there I did hear the charms of the blackbirds and thrushes

Heard by Mr Watts sung by a cowman when he was milking, at Cannon Froome, near Ledbury, Herefordshire, full fifty years ago. A very common song at that time and in that neighbourhood.—Note by Sharp.

[1488 William Henry Watts (72) at Tewkesbury 1908]

(d)

Arise and Pick a Posy

Small birds and turtle doves
In every bush a building
The sun's just a glimmering
Arise my dear.

Arise and pick a posie
Sweet lily pink and rosy
It is the finest flower
That ever I did see

Yes, I will pick a posy
Sweet lily pink and rosy
But there's none so sweet a flower
As the lad I adore.

[1297 Mr Pike at Somerton 1907]

(e)

Rosetta and her Gay Ploughboy

You constant lovers give attention
Whilst to you a tale I'll tell
Concerning of two lovers true
Who in one house for years did dwell

APPENDIX

Rosetta was a farmer's daughter
And always was her parents' joy
Till Cubit in a snare had caught her
With her father's gay ploughboy.

At break of day one summer's morning
William for his house did went
But as he viewed bright Phoebus drorning (*sic*)
He would listen with content.

Till the voice of sweet Rosetta
Who charmed young William's ears with joy
With voice as true she loved young Will
Who was her father's gay ploughboy

She would sit and sing for Sweet William
As she milked her spotted cow
And he would sigh for his Rosetta
All the day while at his plough

And as the evening did reproach
Rosetta trips along with joy
With voice so shrill to meet young Will
Who was her father's gay ploughboy

Her father took her into a dairy
While she sing her tales of love
He fixed his eyes to her surprise
And swear by all the powers above

That he was told this . . . bold
Along with poverty she'd join
And that long time she had been courted
By young William the gay ploughboy

Rosetta says my dearest father
Shall I speak with my courage bold
I milk my cow and have my plough
And values William more than gold

APPENDIX

Then in a cellar he confined her
Where no one could her away
And with delight both day and night
She sighs for Will her gay ploughboy

Fifteen long months on bread and water
Sweet Rosetta was confined
So fast in love did Cubit caught her
No one thing could change her mind

Her father stove with all his might (*sic*)
Her happiness for to destroy
But nothing would Rosetta daunt
She doted on her gay ploughboy

Fifteen long months on bread and water
Sweet Rosetta was confined
Nothing would Rosetta daunt
She doted on her gay ploughboy.

[1511   Job Francis (71) at Shipley 1908]

(*f*)

In Haste

(The Squire and the Maid)

Across the fields the other day
I tripped so light and gay
Our Squire with his dog and gun
He chanced to come that way
He chanced to come that way.
Our Squire with his dog and gun
He chanced to come that way.

O where so fast sweet maid he cried
For I have much to say
I'm going a-walking Sir she said
Be quick for I'm in haste.

APPENDIX

I've seen you much and oft-time wished
Your rosy lips to taste
O then she said we'll have a kiss
Be quick for I'm in haste.

Just as she spoke she saw young Hodge
Come in the neighb'ring gate
He pressed her hand and said dear girl
I'm afraid I've made you wait.

Here is the ring to church we'll go
And joy and love to taste
She leaved the Squire and laughed and said
You see Sir I was in haste

[17 Louie Hooper and Lucy White at Hambridge 1903]

3. This is obviously not a true ballad but an imitation, perhaps influenced by Wordsworth and Coleridge. It has a certain merit of its own.

Squire Curtis

A venerable white haired man
A trusty man and true
Told me this tale as word by word
I tell this tale to you

Squire Curtis rode with his wife
Through the woods far far away
The dusk is drawing round she said
I fear we've gone astray

He spoke no word but still rode on
The stars shone out the sky
At the darkest place he turned him round
'Tis here that you must die

She shrinked once and never again (? shrieked)
He stabbed her with his knife
Once, twice, three times every blow
Enough to take a life

APPENDIX

The grave was ready he laid her in
And filled it up with care
Under the brambles the small fallen leaves
Small sign of grave was there

He rode for an hour at a steady pace
Till unto his house came he
On face on clothes on foot on hand
No stain that eyes could see

He boldly called to his servant man
As he lighted at the door
Say your missus has gone on a sudden journey
May stay for a month or more

In two days I shall follow her
Let her waiting woman know
Sir said the servant man
My lady came in an hour ago

Squire Curtis sat him down in a chair
Never moved neither hand nor head
And then came in the waiting woman
Alas! the day! She said

Alas good Sir said the waiting woman
What ails my mistress dear?
That she sits alone without sign or word
'Tis something wrong I fear.

Her face was white as any corpse
As up the stairs she passed
She never turned she never spoke
And the chamber door is fast

She waits for you; A lie, he shouts
And upon his feet did start
My wife is buried in the brimlin holt
With three wounds in her heart

APPENDIX

They searched the forest in the lantern light
They searched by the dawn of day
At night they found the brimlin brake
And the pit where the body lay.

They carried the murdered woman home
Walking slowly side by side
Squire Curtis was hanged on the gallus tree
And he spoke the truth ere he died

Thus spoke the trusty ancient man
With hair as white as snow
'Twas from his wife the tale he heard
Full fifty years ago.

[1087 Jane Chapman at West Harptree 1906]

4.

Sheep Shearing

Good people all I pray draw near
A true story you soon shall hear
Concerning the sheep that useful thing
That clothes the beggar and the King

And some in silks and satins go
But give to me good woollen clothes
Our bodies from1 the cold to keep

O what is so useful as the sheep
The woollen trade it has increased
Since Joshua stole the golden fleece
            (*two lines missing*)

The infant babe when it is born
Had woollen clothes to keep it warm
And the last garments we shall have
A shroud when we go to the grave

[1754 Mr Beemer (80) at Crowcombe 1908]
    [1] ms. Our brid is for.

INDEX OF FIRST LINES

A brisk young lass so brisk and gay   156
A brisk young lover came a courting me   90
A drowsy young soldier he hung down his head   182
A landlord had one daughter   128
A Lawyer he went out one day   157
A sailor and a soldier was a walking one day   187
A soldier walked in the field one day   122
A squire a squire he lived in the wood   93
A stands for the apple that grows on the tree   63
A sweet country life is most pleasant and charming   235
A venerable white haired man   239
A walking and a talking   97
Abroad as I was walking   230
Across the fields the other day   238
Adieu to old England Adieu and Adieu   61
A-shailing and toiling as I was one day   139
As I crossed over Salisbury Plain   184
As I looked over high Castle wall   149
As I rode over Salisbury Plain   189
As I walked out one evening   197
As I walked out one May morning   79, 80, 106, 109, 126, 192
As I walked out one midsummer's morning   202
As I walked out one morning   70
As I walked out one morning all in the month of May   108
As I walked out one morning fair down by some river side   130
As I was a walking one morning in May   85
As I was a-walking one morning in Spring   198
As I was a-walking one morning in the Spring   145
As I was going to Banbury   69
As I was going to Derby   102
As I was going to Hazelbury   123
As I was walking one midsummer morning   160
As Johnny walked out one fine summer's morn   148
As Willie came by his love he did cry   230

Bessy Bingle had a little pig   74

Come all you gallant poachers   217
Come all you young fellows   87
Come all you young men that are going to be wed   199

Down in my garden there grows a fine flower   110
Down in the meadows the other day   218

Farewell my joy and heart's delight   213
From London Town I went astray   180

Good morning Gossip Joan   117
Good people all I pray draw near   241

INDEX OF FIRST LINES

Have you seen my love pass by 233
Hecketty Pecketty needles and pins 125
He sat my hen a-brood 118
Here's to the maid in Lancashire Town 144
Her master came to her one morning 62
His good old father, his aged mother 188
Hi! Shoo all o' the birds 76

I am a rover and that's well known 185
I am a roving journeyman 186
I am a stranger in this country from America I came 65
I am a tailor by my trade 203
If all those young men were as rushes a growing 119
If young women could build like Blackbirds and Thrushes 120
I had four sisters sailed across the sea 169
I have been a rambling by night and by day 64
I lived in service in Rosemary Lane 181
I'll sing you a song about two true lovers 227
I married a wife and her name was Grace 155
In Kerry city I was born and bred 178
In the Merryshire woods there growed a tree 211
I put my hand all on her toe 113
I saw a snail drive a nail 220
Is she fitting for your wife Billy Boy 75
I so wed the seeds of love 194
It's how can I be merry and free 233
It's of a farmer near London 'tis said 206
It's of a lusty gentleman 104
It's of a sea captain down by the sea side 72
It's of a sea captain who was married of late 191
It's of a wealthy lawyer in Southwark he did dwell 171
It's of two jovial butchers 215
It was an old boatsman down in Dover he did dwell 83
I've been a roving, I've been a roving 129
I went to my love the first to-day 136
I wish I had never known no man at all 129

Jolly old Hawk and his wings was grey 136

Madam I'll present you a fine silken gown 140
Mother I longs to get married 223
My hat is frozen to my head 96
My name it is Jack Hall chimney sweep, chimney sweep 132

Now it's my old man came home one night 167

Oh one day I was taken very ill 101
O it's on the banks of roses where my love and I sit down 115
O my man John what can the matter be 141
Once I was a brisk young bachelor 88
One morn for resurrection as I strayed by the sea-side 235
One morning, one morning, one morning in May 85
On Monday morning I married a wife 164
On the 21st of August in Plymouth Sound we lay 146
On yonder hill there stands a creature 162
O once I was clothèd 175
O once I was courted by a bonny bonny boy 158
O Polly my dear Polly the rout has now begun 125
O the keeper he a shooting goes 138

INDEX OF FIRST LINES

O the prickly briar 153
O 'twas of one summer's morning 233
Our captain cried all hands 165
O what do you think I made out of my red herring's head 179
O when shall us be married 221
O where are you going to my good old man 115

Sailors they are such a sort 189
Sally my dear shall I come to bed to you 119
Small birds and turtle doves 236

The Americans have stole my true love away 98
The red moon is up on the moss-covered mountain 234
The trees that do grow high, and the leaves that do grow green 200
The very first day I got married 151
There was a lady in merry Scotland 225
There was an old couple and they was poor 174
There was an old woman in our town 204
There was a sheep stole from the marsh 198
There was a tree grew in the wood 211
There were seven jolly tradesmen 133
Three cripples from London on the spree 207
Three jolly sailors set out a walking 73
Three maids a milking did go 208
Three pretty maidens a rushing they went 210
'Tis of a pretty female as you shall understand 110
'Twas in the month of May 66
'Twas of a brisk young farmer 77
'Twas Valentine's day come early in the morn 159

Up jumps the salmon 82

When I was bound a prentice 170
When I was young and in my prime 111, 176
Where shall I meet you my pretty little dear 100
Who knocks there? 121

Yonder sits a Spanish lady 163
Young women they'll run like hares on the mountains 119
You constant lovers give attention 236
Young Johnny was a plough boy, so fresh as a rose 68